LIPPINCOTT'S
NEED-TO-KNOW

Nursing
Reference Facts

LIPPINCOTT'S
NEED-TO-KNOW

Nursing
Reference Facts

Maryann Foley, RN, BSN
Clinical Consultant
Flourtown, Pennsylvania

Lippincott
Philadelphia · New York

Acquisitions Editor: Lisa Stead
Assistant Editor: Claudia Vaughn
Production Editor: Virginia Barishek
Production Manager: Helen Ewan
Production Service: P. M. Gordon Associates
Compositor: Circle Graphics
Printer/Binder: R.R. Donnelley & Sons/Crawfordsville
Cover Designer: Jerry Cable
Cover Printer: Lehigh Press

Materials appearing in this book prepared by individuals as part of their
official duties as U.S. Government employees are not covered by the
above-mentioned copyright.

9 8 7 6 5 4 3 2 1

Library of Congress Cataloging-in-Publications Data
Foley, Maryann.
    Lippincott's need-to-know nursing reference facts / Maryann Foley.
      p. cm.
    Includes bibliographical references.
    ISBN 0–7817–1444–3
    1. Reference values (Medicine)—Handbooks, manuals, etc.
  2. Diagnosis, Laboratory—Handbooks, manuals, etc. 3. Nursing—
Handbooks, manuals, etc. I. Title. II. Title: Need-to-know
  reference facts.
    [DNLM: 1. Reference Values. 2. Nursing. WY 16 F663L 1998]
  RB38.2.F65 1998
  610.73—dc21
  DNLM/DLC
  for Library of Congress   97–22695
                                                               CIP

Preface

How to Use

Nurses practicing in today's health care climate are faced with the challenge of performing efficiently, knowledgeably, accurately, and safely. Issues such as health care reform, budget constraints, downsizing, the early discharge of more acutely ill patients, increasing consumer awareness, and health promotion all affect nursing practice. Consequently, information crucial to nursing practice must be readily accessible and available. However, no one person can memorize all the facts needed to function capably in today's health care environment.

Lippincott's Need-to-Know Nursing Reference Facts puts crucial information, such as abbreviations, laboratory values, and normal and abnormal assessment findings, together in one convenient source. This practical, comprehensive, yet portable resource serves as a quick reference for that essential, need-to-know material that may be difficult to memorize or hard to find.

Lippincott's Need-to-Know Nursing Reference Facts is designed for any nurse, whether a student, new graduate, or experienced practitioner, regardless of the practice setting. The information contained in this resource puts hundreds of different facts, figures, charts, and numbers at the nurse's fingertips. Its concise, streamlined, yet highly usable approach eliminates the frills found in larger texts while still focusing on the essential material.

Lippincott's Need-to-Know Nursing Reference Facts is divided into 12 chapters. Each chapter deals with a specific area of care or body system.

Chapter 1 focuses on the fundamental concepts necessary for all nursing practice. Reference facts for this chapter include medical terminology, abbreviations, body planes and positions, and assessment parameters. In addition, the most recent information on NANDA taxonomy and standard precautions is presented.

Chapter 2 focuses on pharmacology. Reference facts for this chapter include equivalents and conversions, body surface nomograms, equianalgesic dosages, drug compatibilities, IV flow rates, and IV catheter maintenance guidelines. In addition, laboratory values for commonly monitored drugs and peak and trough levels for commonly used antibiotics are included.

Chapters 3 through 12 present reference facts for specific body systems. Chapter 3 focuses on respiratory function. Reference facts for this chapter include respiratory landmarks, normal and abnormal breath sounds, oxygen administration devices and concentrations, arterial blood gases and their interpretation, and respiratory acid–base imbalances. Laboratory values for pulmonary function tests are also listed.

Chapter 4 focuses on cardiovascular function. Reference facts for this chapter include cardiac landmarks, assessment of heart sounds and jugular venous distention, ECG lead placement, diagnostic and hemodynamic assessment of myocardial infarction, and heart murmur grading. Laboratory values for lipoprotein tests also are included.

Chapter 5 focuses on neurologic function. Reference facts for this chapter include assessments for cranial nerve function, mental status, Glasgow Coma Scale, and deep tendon reflexes. Illustrations of posturing positions as well as laboratory values for normal cerebrospinal fluid also are included.

Chapter 6 focuses on gastrointestinal function. Reference facts in this chapter include abdominal quadrants and regions, nutritional aspects, such as special diets and enteral and parenteral nutrition, and treatments such as commonly used enema solutions and gastrointestinal intubation. Laboratory values for liver function tests also are provided.

Chapter 7 focuses on fluid and electrolyte balance. Reference facts for this chapter include assessment parameters, normal electrolyte values, and signs and symptoms of water, electrolyte, and acid–base imbalances.

Chapter 8 focuses on renal and urologic function. Reference facts for this chapter include normal urine characteristics, renal function tests, categories of renal failure, and recommended dosages of antibiotics for patients with renal failure. Laboratory values for routine urinalysis and blood urea nitrogen (BUN) also are included.

Chapter 9 focuses on endocrine and metabolic function. Reference facts for this chapter include clinical manifestations of endocrine dysfunction, diabetes classification and complications, insulin types and oral antidiabetic agents, signs and symptoms of DKA, HHNS, and insulin reaction, systematic assessment of ABGs, and changes occurring in acid–base imbalances. Laboratory values for fasting blood sugar, glycosylated hemoglobin, and glucose tolerance tests also are included.

Chapter 10 focuses on hematologic and immunologic function. Reference facts for this chapter include characteristics of white blood cells (WBC), blood groups, ABO and Rh compatibility, reactions to blood transfusions, adult immunizations, opportunistic infections, sexually transmitted diseases, and infectious diseases. Laboratory values for bone marrow aspirations, differential white blood cell count, red blood cell count, hemoglobin and hematocrit, coagulant factors, immunoglobulins, and lymphocyte immunophenotyping also are presented.

Chapter 11 focuses on musculoskeletal function. Reference facts for this chapter include skeletal divisions, major bones and muscles of the body, joint types, body movement terminology, and range of motion. Types of fractures also are included.

Chapter 12 focuses on integumentary function. Reference facts for this chapter include skin color assessment, types of skin lesions and wounds, common pressure points, stages of wound healing and pressure sores, and temperatures for heat and cold applications. Burn assessment, including characteristics, the rule of nines, and the Lund and Browder scale also are provided.

Both practicing nurses and nursing students will find *Lippincott's Need-to-Know Nursing Reference Facts* to be a current, accurate, and complete reference for clinical practice or class, providing essential information needed for competent and skillful caregiving.

Contents

CHAPTER 3
Respiratory Reference Facts   57

CHAPTER 4
Cardiovascular Reference Facts   69

CHAPTER 5
Neurologic Reference Facts   77

CHAPTER 6
Gastrointestinal Reference Facts   89

CHAPTER 7
Fluid and Electrolyte Reference Facts   107

CHAPTER 8
Renal and Urologic Reference Facts   149

CHAPTER 9
Endocrine and Metabolic Reference
Facts   165

CHAPTER 10
Hematologic and Immunologic
Reference Facts   187

CHAPTER 11
Musculoskeletal Reference Facts   241

CHAPTER 12
Integumentary Reference Facts   259

CHAPTER 1

Foundational Concepts of Reference Facts

TABLE 1-1 Medical Terminology: Prefixes, Roots, and Suffixes
••

Medical terms are made up of components that are derived mostly from Latin or Greek. The root is the main part of the word. Prefixes precede the root and suffixes follow the root to modify its meaning. The roots are presented here with combining vowels that are used to ease pronunciation when a suffix is added.

PREFIXES

Prefix	Meaning	Prefix	Meaning
a-, an-	without, not	hyper-	high, excessive
ab-	away from	hypo-	under, decreased
acro-	extremity	in-, im-	in, within
ad-	to, toward	in-, im-	not
ambi-	both	infra-	below
ante-	before	inter-	between
anti-	against	intra-	within
auto-	self	iso-	equal, same
bi-	two, double	juxta-	near
brady-	slow	leuk/o-	white, colorless
circum-	around	macro-	large
co-	together	mal-	bad, poor
contra-	against	melan/o-	black, dark
de-	without, removal	mega/lo-	large, enlarged
di-	two, twice	mes/o-	middle
dia-	through	meta-	beyond, over, change
diplo-	double, two		
dis-	removal, separation	micr/o-	small, one millionth
dys-	abnormal, difficult, painful		
		mon/o-	one
ecto-	outside	multi-	many
endo-	within	neo-	new
epi-	above	noct/i-	night
eryth/r/o-	red	non-	not
eu-	normal, good, true	olig/o-	little, deficiency
ex/o-	out, out of	ortho-	straight, correct
extra-	outside, in addition to	pan-	all
		para-	beside, near
hemi-	half	per-	by, through
hetero-	other, different	peri-	around
homo-, homeo-	same	poly-	many

(continued)

TABLE 1-1 Medical Terminology: Prefixes, Roots, and Suffixes (Continued)

PREFIXES

Prefix	Meaning	Prefix	Meaning
post-	after, behind	sub-	below, under
pre-	before	super-	above, excessive
prim/i-	first	supra-	above
pro-	before	syn-, sym-	together
pseud/o-	false	tachy-	fast
quad/r/i-	four	trans-	through, across
re-	back, again	tri-	three
retro-	backward, behind	ultra-	beyond
scler/o-	hard, hardening	un-	not
semi-	half	uni-	one

ROOTS

Root	Meaning	Root	Meaning
aden/o	gland	cyst/o	sac, bladder
angi/o	vessel	cyt/o	cell
arteri/o	artery	derm, dermat/o	skin
arthr/o	joint	encephal/o	brain
audi/o	hearing	enter/o	intestine
bio	life	gastr/o	stomach
blast/o	immature form, growing form	genesis	origin
		glomerul/o	glomerulus
brachi/o	arm	gloss/o	tongue
bronch/o, bronchi/o	bronchus	hem/o, hemat/o	blood
		hepat/o	liver
carcin/o	cancer	hist/o	tissue
cardi/o	heart	hydro/o	water, fluid
cerebr/o	brain	hyster/o	uterus
cephal/o	head	ile/o	ileum
cervic/o	neck, cervix	ili/o	ilium
chol/e	bile	kerat/o	cornea, horny layer of the skin
cholecyst/o	gallbladder		
chondr/o	cartilage	labi/o	lip, labium
cleid/o	clavicle	lact/o	milk
col/o	colon	laryng/o	larynx
colp/o	vagina	lith/o	stone
cost/o	rib	lymph/o	lymph
crani/o	skull	mast/o	breast

TABLE 1-1 Medical Terminology: Prefixes, Roots, and Suffixes (Continued)

ROOTS

Root	Meaning	Root	Meaning
medull/o	central part, medulla oblongata	phag/o	eating
		phak/o, phac/o	lens of the eye
men/o	menses	phleb/o	vein
mening/o	meninges	pneum/o,	lung, air,
metr/o	uterus	pneumon/o	breathing
my/o	muscle	proct/o	rectum
myc/o	fungus	psych/o	mind
myel/o	marrow, spinal cord	ptosis	dropping
myring/o	tympanic membrane	py/o	pus
		pyel/o	pelvis, renal pelvis
nas/o	nose	pylor/o	pylorus
necr/o	death	rachi/o	spine
nephr/o	kidney	ren/o	kidney
neur/o	nerve	rhin/o	nose
ocul/o	eye	salping/o	tube, oviduct
odont/o	tooth	scler/o	hardening
onc/o	tumor, swelling	splen/o	spleen
onych/o	nail	thorac/o	chest, thorax
oo	egg, ovum	thromb/o	blood clot
oophor/o	ovary	tox/o, toxic/o	poison
ophthalm/o	eye	trache/o	trachea
orchi/o, orchid/o	testis	trich/o	hair
		ureter/o	ureter
os, oste/o	bone	urethr/o	urethra
ot/o	ear	ur/o	urine
ovari/o	ovary	vas/o	vessel, duct
path/o	disease	vesic/o	urinary bladder
ped/o	child, foot		

SUFFIXES

Suffix	Meaning	Suffix	Meaning
-algia	pain	-ectasis	dilation, stretching
-cele	tumor, hernia, swelling	-ectomy	excision
		-emia	blood
-centesis	puncture, tap	-esthesia	pertaining to sensation
-cide	killing		

(continued)

TABLE 1-1   Medical Terminology: Prefixes, Roots, and Suffixes (Continued)

SUFFIXES

Suffix	Meaning	Suffix	Meaning
-form	shaped like	-phil, -philic	attracting
-gen,-genic	formation, origin, producing	-plasia	formation, molding
-gram	record	-plasty	plastic repair
-graph	recording instrument	-plegia	paralysis
		-pnea	breathing
-graphy	recording of data	-poiesis	formation, production
-iasis	condition		
-ism	condition	-ptosis	dropping
-itis	inflammation	-rhage, -rhagia	bursting forth
-logy	study	-rhaphy	surgical repair
-lysis	separation, disintegration	-rhea	discharge
		-rhexis	rupture
-malacia	softening	-scope	instrument for examining
-megaly	enlargement		
-meter	measuring instrument	-scopy	visual examination
-metry	measurement	-stasis	stoppage of flow
-odynia	pain	-stomy	surgical formation of an opening
-oid	like, resembling		
-oma	tumor	-tomy	incision into
-osis	condition	-trophy	nourishing
-pathy	disease	-tropic	acting on
-penia	lack of	-tripsy	crushing
-pexy	surgical fixation	-uresis	urination
-phagia	eating	-uria	urine

TABLE 1-2 Commonly Used Abbreviations

Abbreviation	Meaning	Abbreviation	Meaning
ā	before	HOB	head of bed
abd	abdomen	h.s.	bedtime
ac	before meals		(hour of sleep)
ADLs	activities of daily living	hx	history
		I & O	intake & output
ad lib	as needed	IM	intramuscular
adm.	admitted, admission	IV	intravenous
		kg	kilogram
amp.	ampule	KVO	keep vein open
ant.	anterior	L	left; liter
AP	anterior–posterior	lat	lateral
ax.	axillary	MAE	moves all extremities
b.i.d.	twice a day		
BP	blood pressure	mg	milligram
BR	bed rest	ml, mL	milliliter
BRP	bathroom privileges		(1 mL = 1 cc)
		NAD	no apparent distress
C	Centigrade, Celsius		
c̄	with	NG	nasogastric
caps	capsule	noc	night
C.C.	chief complaint	NPO	nothing by mouth
cc	cubic centimeter (1 cc = 1 mL)	os	mouth
		OOB	out of bed
CVP	central venous pressure	oz	ounce
		p̄	after
c/o	complains of	p.c.	after meals
D/C	discontinue	post	posterior
disch, DC	discharge	prep	preparation
drsg	dressing	prn	when necessary
dr	dram	q̄, q	every
elix	elixir	q̄, 2 (3, 4, etc.) hours	every 2 (3, 4, etc.) hours
ext	extract or external		
F	Fahrenheit	qd	every day
fx.	fracture, fractional	qh	every hour
g, gm	gram	q.i.d.	four times a day
gr	grain	q.o.d.	every other day
gtt	drop	q.s.	quantity sufficient
"H," SC, or sub q	hypodermic or subcutaneous	R/O	rule out
		ROM	range of motion
h	hour	s̄	without

(continued)

TABLE 1-2 Commonly Used Abbreviations (Continued)

Abbreviation	Meaning	Abbreviation	Meaning
SBA	stand by assistance	TPN	total parenteral nutrition, hyper-alimentation
SC	subcutaneous		
SL	sublingual		
SOB	shortness of breath	TPR	temperature, pulse, respiration
sol, soln	solution		
spec	specimen	tsp	teaspoon
S/P	status post	TO	telephone order
sp. gr.	specific gravity	TWE	tap water enema
S.S.E.	soapsuds edema	VO	verbal order
ss	one-half	VS	vital signs
stat	immediately	VSS	vital signs stable
tab	tablet	W/C	wheelchair
t.i.d.	three times a day	WNL	within normal limits
tinct or tr.	tincture		
TKO	to keep open		

SELECTED ABBREVIATIONS USED FOR SPECIFIC DESCRIPTIONS

Abbreviation	Meaning	Abbreviation	Meaning
AKA	above-knee amputation	D_5W	5% dextrose in water
ASCVD	arteriosclerotic cardiovascular disease	FUO	fever of unknown origin
		GB	gallbladder
ASHD	arteriosclerotic heart disease	GI	gastrointestinal
		GYN	gynecology
BKA	below-knee amputation	H_2O_2	hydrogen peroxide
		HA	hyperalimenta-tion; headache
ca	cancer		
chest clear to A & P	chest clear to auscultation & percussion	HCVD	hypertensive cardiovascular disease
CMS	circulation, movement, sensation	HEENT	head, ear, eye, nose, throat
CNS	central nervous system	HVD	hypertensive vascular disease
		ICU	intensive care unit
DJD	degenerative joint disease	I & D	incision and drainage
DOE	dyspnea on exertion	LLE	left lower extremity
DT's	delirium tremens	LLQ	left lower quadrant

TABLE 1-2 Commonly Used Abbreviations (Continued)

....

Abbreviation	Meaning	Abbreviation	Meaning
LOC	level of consciousness; laxatives of choice	PM & R	physical medicine & rehabilitation
LMP	last menstrual period	Psych	psychology; psychiatric
LUE	left upper extremity	PT	physical therapy
LUQ	left upper quadrant	RL (or LR)	Ringer's lactate, lactated Ringer's
MI	myocardial infarction	RLE	right lower extremity
Neuro	neurology; neurosurgery	RLQ	right lower quadrant
NS	normal saline	RR, PAR	recovery room, postanesthesia room
Nsy	nursery		
NWB	non–weight-bearing	RUE	right upper extremity
O.D.	right eye	RUQ	right upper quadrant
O.S.	left eye	Rx	prescription
O.U.	each eye	STSG	split-thickness skin graft
OPD	outpatient department	Surg	surgery, surgical
ORIF	open reduction internal fixation	T & A	tonsillectomy & adenoidectomy
Ortho	orthopedics	THR, TJR	total hip replacement; total joint replacement
OT	occupational therapy		
PE	physical examination	URI	upper respiratory infection
PERRLA	pupils equal, round, & react to light and accommodation	UTI	urinary tract infection
		vag	vaginal
PID	pelvic inflammatory disease	VD	venereal disease
PI	present illness	WNWD	well-nourished, well-developed

SELECTED ABBREVIATIONS RELATED TO COMMON DIAGNOSTIC TESTS

BE	barium enema	Ca^{++}	calcium
B.M.R.	basal metabolism rate	CAT	computed axial tomography

(continued)

TABLE 1-2 Commonly Used Abbreviations (Continued)

Abbreviation	Meaning	Abbreviation	Meaning
CBC	complete blood count	IVP	intravenous pyelogram
Cl⁻	chloride	K⁺	potassium
C & S	culture & sensitivity	LP	lumbar puncture
Dx	diagnosis	MRI	magnetic resonance imaging
ECG, EKG	electrocardiogram	Na⁺	sodium
EEG	electroencephalogram	RBC	red blood cell
FBS	fasting blood sugar	UGI	upper gastrointestinal x-ray
hct	hematocrit	UA	urinalysis
Hgb	hemoglobin	WBC	white blood cell

COMMONLY USED SYMBOLS

>	greater than	+	positive
<	less than	−	negative
=	equal to	±	positive or negative
≈	approximately equal to	F_1	first filial generation
≤	less than or equal to	F_2	second filial generation
≥	greater than or equal to	PO_2	partial pressure of oxygen
↑	increased	PCO_2	partial pressure of carbon dioxide
↓	decreased		
♀	female	:	ratio
♂	male	∴	therefore
°	degree	%	percent
#	number or pound	2°	secondary to
×	times	Δ	change
@	at		

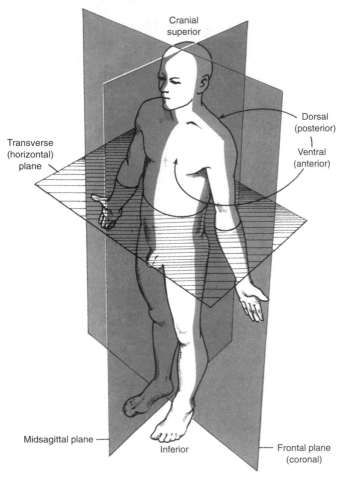

FIGURE 1-1 Body planes and directions.

TABLE 1-3 Body Planes and Directions

Position	Definition	Examples
Superior	"Above" or in a higher position	The knee is superior to the toes but inferior to the femur.
Inferior	"Below" or in a lower position	The lips are inferior to the nose but superior to the chin.
Cranial	In or near the head	The brain is in the cranial cavity.
Caudal	Near the lower end of the body, (ie, near the end of the spine), "tail"	The buttocks, the muscles on which we sit, are located at the caudal end of the body
Anterior or ventral	Toward the front or "belly" surface of the body	The nose is on the anterior, or ventral, surface of the head.
Posterior or dorsal	Toward the back of the body	The calf is on the posterior, or dorsal, surface of the leg.
Medial	Nearer the midline	The nose is medial to the eyes.
Lateral	Farther from the midline, toward the side	The ears are lateral to the nose.
Internal	Deeper within the body	The stomach is an internal body organ.
External	Toward the outer surface of the body	The skin covers the external surface of the body.
Proximal	Nearest the origin of a part	In the upper extremity (arm), the upper arm above the elbow is proximal to the forearm below.

Distal	Farthest from the origin of a part	In the lower extremity (leg), the lower leg below the knee is distal to the thigh.
Central	Situated at or pertaining to the center	The brain and the spinal cord are part of the central nervous system.
Peripheral	Situated at or pertaining to the outward part of a surface	The peripheral nerves go out to the body parts and return to the central nervous system.
Parietal	Pertaining to the sides or the walls of a cavity	The walls of the abdominal cavity are lined with a membrane called the parietal peritoneum.
Visceral	Pertaining to the organs within a cavity	The stomach and intestines are visceral organs in the abdominal cavity.
Supine	Lying with the face upward	A person lying on the dorsal surface of the body, or on the back, is supine.
Prone	Lying with the face downward	A person lying on the ventral surface, or the front of the body, is prone.
Deep	Away from the surface	The knife wound was deep in the abdomen.
Superficial	On or near the surface	The child had a superficial cut.

A. High Fowler's

B. Supine

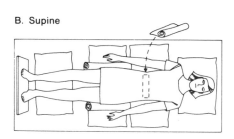

C. Prone

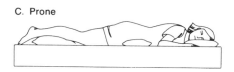

D. Side-lying

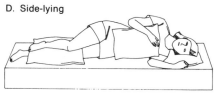

FIGURE 1-2 Body positioning.

E. Sim's

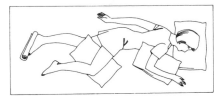

F. Lithotomy

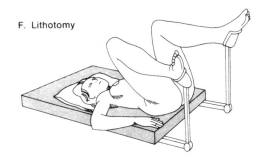

G. Dorsal Recumbent

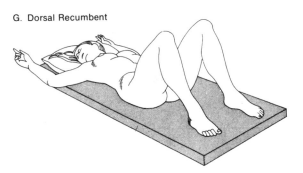

FIGURE 1-2 (Continued)

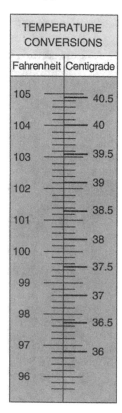

FIGURE 1-3 Temperature conversion chart. To change Celsius into Fahrenheit, multiply the Celsius reading by ⅗ and add 32 to the result.

$$F = (9/5 \times C°) + 32°$$

To change Fahrenheit into Celsius, subtract 32 from the Fahrenheit reading and multiply the result by ⅚.

$$C = (F° - 32°) \times 5/9$$

TABLE 1-4 Height–Weight Tables

Men

Height Feet	Inches	Small Frame	Medium Frame	Large Frame
5	2	128–134	131–141	138–150
5	3	130–136	133–143	140–153
5	4	132–138	135–145	142–156
5	5	134–140	137–148	144–160
5	6	136–142	139–151	146–164
5	7	138–145	142–154	149–168
5	8	140–148	145–157	152–172
5	9	142–151	148–160	155–176
5	10	144–154	151–163	158–180
5	11	146–157	154–166	161–184
6	0	149–160	157–170	164–188
6	1	152–164	160–174	168–192
6	2	155–168	164–178	172–197
6	3	158–172	167–182	176–202
6	4	162–176	171–187	181–207

Women

Height Feet	Inches	Small Frame	Medium Frame	Large Frame
4	10	102–111	109–121	118–131
4	11	103–113	111–123	120–134
5	0	104–115	113–126	122–137
5	1	106–118	115–129	125–140
5	2	108–121	118–132	128–143
5	3	111–124	121–135	131–147
5	4	114–127	124–138	134–151
5	5	117–130	127–141	137–155
5	6	120–133	130–144	140–159
5	7	123–136	133–147	143–163
5	8	126–139	136–150	146–167
5	9	129–142	139–153	149–170
5	10	132–145	142–156	152–173
5	11	135–148	145–159	155–176
6	0	138–151	148–162	158–179

Weight according to frame (ages 25–59) for men wearing indoor clothing weighing 5 lbs, shoes with 1-in. heels; for women wearing indoor clothing weighing 3 lbs., shoes with 1-in. heels.
(Courtesy Metropolitan Life Insurance Company.)

TABLE 1-5 Normal Vital Sign Ranges across the Lifespan

	Pulse	Respirations	Temperature (°F)	Blood Pressure (mm Hg)	
				Systolic	*Diastolic*
Newborn (>96 h)	70–190	30–60	96–99.5	60–90	20–60
Infant (>1 mo)	80–160	30–60	99.4–99.7	74–100	50–70
Toddler	80–130	24–40	99–99.7	80–112	50–80
Preschooler	80–120	22–34	98.6–99	82–110	50–78
School-age	75–110	18–30	98–98.6	84–120	54–80
Adolescent	60–90	12–20	97–99	94–140	62–88
Adult	60–100	12–20	97–99	90–140	60–90
Older adult (>70 y)	60–100	12–20	96–99	90–140	60–90

TABLE 1-6 Pulse Quality Rating Scale

0	No pulse detected
1+	Thready, weak pulse, easily obliterated with pressure; pulse may come and go
2+	Pulse difficult to palpate; may be obliterated with pressure
3+	Normal pulse
4+	Bounding, hyperactive pulse; easily palpated and cannot be obliterated

TABLE 1-7 Recommended Bladder Dimensions for Blood Pressure Cuffs

Arm Circumference at Midpoint* (cm)	Cuff Type	Bladder Width (cm)	Bladder Length (cm)
5–7.5	Newborn	3	5
7.5–13	Infant	5	8
13–20	Child	8	13
24–32	Adult	13	24
32–42	Wide adult	17	32
42–50†	Thigh	20	42

* Midpoint of arm is defined as half the distance from acromion to olecranon. Use nonstretchable metal tape.

† In persons with very large limbs, indirect blood pressure should be measured in leg or forearm.

From Recommendations for Human Blood Pressure Determination by Sphygmomanometers, American Heart Association, 1987.

TABLE 1-8 Characteristics of Percussion Tones

Tone	Quality	Pitch	Intensity	Location
Flatness	Extreme dullness	High	Soft	Sternum, thigh
Dullness	Thud-like	Medium	Medium	Liver, diaphragm
Resonance	Hollow	Low	Loud	Normal lung
Hyperresonance	Booming	Very low	Very loud	Emphysematous lung
Tympany	Musical, drum-like	High	Loud	Air-filled stomach

TABLE 1-9 **NANDA Taxonomy**

• •

This list represents the NANDA-approved nursing diagnoses for clinical use and testing (1994).

PATTERN I: EXCHANGING

1.1.2.1	Altered Nutrition: More than body requirements
1.1.2.2	Altered Nutrition: Less than body requirements
1.1.2.3	Altered Nutrition: Potential for more than body requirements
1.2.1.1	Risk for Infection
1.2.2.1	Risk for Altered Body Temperature
1.2.2.2	Hypothermia
1.2.2.3	Hyperthermia
1.2.2.4	Ineffective Thermoregulation
1.2.3.1	Dysreflexia
1.3.1.1	Constipation
1.3.1.1.1	Perceived Constipation
1.3.1.1.2	Colonic Constipation
1.3.1.2	Diarrhea
1.3.1.3	Bowel Incontinence
1.3.2	Altered Urinary Elimination
1.3.2.1.1	Stress Incontinence
1.3.2.1.2	Reflex Incontinence
1.3.2.1.3	Urge Incontinence
1.3.2.1.4	Functional Incontinence
1.3.2.1.5	Total Incontinence
1.3.2.2	Urinary Retention
1.4.1.1	Altered (Specify Type) Tissue Perfusion (Renal, cerebral, cardiopulmonary, gastrointestinal, peripheral)
1.4.1.2.1	Fluid Volume Excess
1.4.1.2.2.1	Fluid Volume Deficit
1.4.1.2.2.2	Risk for Fluid Volume Deficit
1.4.2.1	Decreased Cardiac Output
1.5.1.1	Impaired Gas Exchange
1.5.1.2	Ineffective Airway Clearance
1.5.1.3	Ineffective Breathing Pattern
1.5.1.3.1	Inability to Sustain Spontaneous Ventilation
1.5.1.3.2	Dysfunctional Ventilatory Weaning Response (DVWR)
1.6.1	Risk for Injury
1.6.1.1	Risk for Suffocation
1.6.1.2	Risk for Poisoning
1.6.1.3	Risk for Trauma
1.6.1.4	Risk for Aspiration
1.6.1.5	Risk for Disuse Syndrome
1.6.2	Altered Protection
1.6.2.1	Impaired Tissue Integrity

TABLE 1-9 NANDA Taxonomy (Continued)

••

1.6.2.1.1   Altered Oral Mucous Membrane
1.6.2.1.2.1   Impaired Skin Integrity
1.6.2.1.2.2   Risk for Impaired Skin Integrity
    #1.7.1   Decreased Adaptive Capacity: Intracranial
    #1.8   Energy Field Disturbance

PATTERN 2: COMMUNICATING

2.1.1.1   Impaired Verbal Communication

PATTERN 3: RELATING

    3.1.1   Impaired Social Interaction
    3.1.2   Social Isolation
    #3.1.3   Risk for Loneliness
    3.2.1   Altered Role Performance
  3.2.1.1.1   Altered Parenting
  3.2.1.1.2   Risk for Altered Parenting
#3.2.1.1.2.1   Risk for Altered Parent/Infant/Child Attachment
  3.2.1.2.1   Sexual Dysfunction
    3.2.2   Altered Family Processes
    3.2.2.1   Caregiver Role Strain
    3.2.2.2   Risk for Caregiver Role Strain
  #3.2.2.3.1   Altered Family Process: Alcoholism
    3.2.3.1   Parental Role Conflict
      3.3   Altered Sexuality Patterns

PATTERN 4: VALUING

    4.1.1   Spiritual Distress (distress of the human spirit)
    #4.2   Potential for Enhanced Spiritual Well Being

PATTERN 5: CHOOSING

  5.1.1.1   Ineffective Individual Coping
  5.1.1.1.1   Impaired Adjustment
  5.1.1.1.2   Defensive Coping
  5.1.1.1.3   Ineffective Denial
  5.1.2.1.1   Ineffective Family Coping: Disabling
  5.1.2.1.2   Ineffective Family Coping: Compromised
  #5.1.3.1   Potential for Enhanced Community Coping
  #5.1.3.2   Ineffective Community Coping
  5.1.2.2   Family Coping: Potential for Growth
    5.2.1   Ineffective Management of Therapeutic Regimen (Individuals)
  5.2.1.1   Noncompliance (Specify)

(continued)

TABLE 1-9 NANDA Taxonomy (Continued)

••

#5.2.2 Ineffective Management of Therapeutic Regimen: Families
#5.2.3 Ineffective Management of Therapeutic Regimen: Community
#5.2.4 Ineffective Management of Therapeutic Regimen: Individual
5.3.1.1 Decisional Conflict (Specify)
5.4 Health Seeking Behaviors (Specify)

PATTERN 6: MOVING

6.1.1.1 Impaired Physical Mobility
6.1.1.1.1 Risk for Peripheral Neurovascular Dysfunction
#6.1.1.1.2 Risk for Perioperative Positioning Injury
6.1.1.2 Activity Intolerance
6.1.1.2.1 Fatigue
6.1.1.3 Risk for Activity Intolerance
6.2.1 Sleep Pattern Disturbance
6.3.1.1 Diversional Activity Deficit
6.4.1.1 Impaired Home Maintenance Management
6.4.2 Altered Health Maintenance
6.5.1 Feeding Self Care Deficit
6.5.1.1 Impaired Swallowing
6.5.1.2 Ineffective Breastfeeding
6.5.1.2.1 Interrupted Breastfeeding
6.5.1.3 Effective Breastfeeding
6.5.1.4 Ineffective Infant Feeding Pattern
6.5.2 Bathing/Hygiene Self Care Deficit
6.5.3 Dressing/Grooming Self Care Deficit
6.5.4 Toileting Self Care Deficit
6.6 Altered Growth and Development
6.7 Relocation Stress Syndrome
#6.8.1 Risk for Disorganized Infant Behavior
#6.8.2 Disorganized Infant Behavior
#6.8.3 Potential for Enhanced Organized Infant Behavior

PATTERN 7: PERCEIVING

7.1.1 Body Image Disturbance
7.1.2 Self Esteem Disturbance
7.1.2.1 Chronic Low Self Esteem
7.1.2.2 Situational Low Self Esteem
7.1.3 Personal Identity Disturbance
7.2 Sensory/Perceptual Alterations (Specify) (Visual, auditory, kinesthetic, gustatory, tactile, olfactory)
7.2.1.1 Unilateral Neglect
7.3.1 Hopelessness
7.3.2 Powerlessness

TABLE 1-9 NANDA Taxonomy (Continued)

PATTERN 8: KNOWING

8.1.1 Knowledge Deficit (Specify)
#8.2.1 Impaired Environmental Interpretation Syndrome
#8.2.2 Acute Confusion
#8.2.3 Chronic Confusion
  8.3 Altered Thought Processes
#8.3.1 Impaired Memory

PATTERN 9: FEELING

9.1.1 Pain
9.1.1.1 Chronic Pain
9.2.1.1 Dysfunctional Grieving
9.2.1.2 Anticipatory Grieving
  9.2.2 Risk for Violence: Self-directed or directed at others
9.2.2.1 Risk for Self-Mutilation
  9.2.3 Post-Trauma Response
9.2.3.1 Rape-Trauma Syndrome
9.2.3.1.1 Rape-Trauma Syndrome: Compound Reaction
9.2.3.1.2 Rape-Trauma Syndrome: Silent Reaction
  9.3.1 Anxiety
  9.3.2 Fear

New diagnoses added in 1994

TABLE 1-10 Standard Precautions

- Wear clean gloves when touching:

  blood, body fluids, secretions and excretions, and items containing these body substances

  mucous membranes

  nonintact skin

- Perform handwashing immediately:

  when there is direct contact with blood, body fluids, secretions and excretions, and contaminated items

  after removing gloves

  between patient contacts

- Wear a mask, eye protection, face shield:

  during procedures and patient care activities that are likely to generate splashes or sprays of blood, body fluids, secretions, and excretions

- Wear a cover gown:

  during procedures and patient care activities that are likely to generate splashes or sprays of blood, body fluids, secretions or excretions, or cause soiling of clothing

- Remove soiled protective items promptly when the potential for contact with reservoirs of pathogens is no longer present.

- Clean and reprocess all equipment before reuse by another patient.

- Discard all single-use items promptly in appropriate containers that prevent contact with blood, body fluids, secretions and excretions, contamination of clothing, and transfer of microorganisms to other patients and the environment.

- Handle, transport, and process linen soiled with blood, body fluids, and secretions and excretions in such a way as to prevent skin and mucous membrane exposures, contamination of clothing, or transfer to other patients and the environment.

- Prevent injuries with used needles, scalpels, and other sharp devices by:

  never removing, recapping, bending, or breaking used needles

24

never pointing the needle toward a body part

using a one-handed "scoop" method, special syringes with a retractable protective guard or shield for enclosing a needle, or blunt-point needles

depositing disposable and reusable syringes and needles in puncture-resistant containers

- Use a private room or consult with an infection control professional for the care of patients who contaminate the environment, or who cannot or do not assist with appropriate hygiene or environmental cleanliness measures.

TRANSMISSION-BASED PRECAUTIONS*

Type of Precaution	Patient Placement	Protection	Examples of Diseases
Airborne	Private room Negative air pressure† Discharge of room air to environment or filtered before being circulated	Follow Standard Precautions. Wear a mask for airborne pathogens or particulate air filter respirator in the case of tuberculosis. Place a mask on the patient if transport is required.	Tuberculosis Measles Chickenpox
Droplet	Private room, or in a room with a similarly infected patient(s) or one in which there is at least 3 feet between other patient(s) and visitors	Follow Standard Precautions. Wear a mask when entering the room, but especially when within 3 feet of the infected patient. Place a mask on the patient if a transport is required.	Influenza Rubella Streptococcal pneumonia Meningococcal meningitis

(continued)

TABLE 1-10 **Standard Precautions** (Continued)

TRANSMISSION-BASED PRECAUTIONS*

Type of Precaution	Patient Placement	Protection	Examples of Diseases
Contact	Private room, or in a room with similarly infected patient(s), or Consult with an infection control professional if the above options are not available.	Follow Standard Precautions. Don gloves before entering the room. Remove gloves before leaving the room. Change gloves after contact with infective material. Perform handwashing with an antimicrobial agent immediately after removing gloves. Wear a gown when entering the room if there is the possibility that your clothing will touch the patient or items in	Gastrointestinal, respiratory, skin, or wound infections that are drug resistant Acute diarrhea Draining abscess

the room, or if the patient is incontinent or has diarrhea, an ileostomy, a colostomy, or wound drainage not contained by a dressing.

Avoid transporting the patient, but, if required, use precautions that minimize transmission.

Clean bedside equipment and patient care items daily.

Use items such as a stethoscope, sphygmomanometer and the other assessment tools exclusively for the infected patient and terminally disinfect them when precautions are no longer necessary.

† Negative air pressure pulls air from the hall into the room when the door is opened, as opposed to positive air pressure, which pulls room air into the hall.

* Source: Centers for Disease Control and Prevention. Draft guideline for isolation precautions in hospitals; notice. Federal Register November 7, 1994;59:55552–55570.

CHAPTER 2

Pharmacology
Reference Facts

TABLE 2-1 Equivalents and Conversions
• •

EQUIVALENTS
Metric Units

The metric system, developed by the French, uses the *meter* as the basic unit. The metric system is a decimal system, with prefixes that designate the various multiples or divisibles of 10. The most commonly used prefixes in medicine are

Milli, which means one one-thousandth (0.001)
Centi, which means one one-hundredth (0.01)
Kilo, which means one thousand (1000)

These prefixes may be affixed to any of the three basic units of measurement, which are

Meter (m), the unit of length
Gram (g), the unit of weight
Liter (L), the unit of volume

Therefore

1 millimeter (mm) = 0.001 m
1 milligram (mg) = 0.001 g
1 milliliter (mL) = 0.001 L
1 kilometer (km) = 1000 m
1 kilogram (kg) = 1000 g
1 kiloliter (kl) = 1000 L

Length

The meter (a little longer than a yard) and the kilometer (about 0.6 mile) seldom are used in medicine or nursing. The commonly used measure of length is 1 centimeter (cm) = 0.01 m = about 0.4 inch.

Volume

The most frequently used measures of volume are the *liter* and the *milliliter.* Some useful equivalents to know are

1000 milliliters (mL) = 1 liter (L)
1000 cubic centimeters (cc) = 1 liter (L)
1 milliliter (mL) = 1 cc

(continued)

TABLE 2-1 Equivalents and Conversions (Continued)

••

Weight

The gram designates the weight of 1 mL of distilled water to 4°C. The most frequently used units of weight are

1,000,000 micrograms (mcg or μg) = 1 gram (g)
1000 micrograms (mcg) = 1 milligram (mg)
1000 milligrams (mg) = 1 gram (g)
1000 grams (g) = 1 kilogram (kg) = 2.2 pounds (lb)

Metric Units and Their Household Equivalents

Household measurement is inaccurate, with wide variations in the size of teaspoons, teacups, and so forth. The generally accepted household measures are

60 drops (gtt) = 1 teaspoon (tsp or t)
3 tsp = 1 tablespoon (Tbs or T)
12 Tbs = 1 teacup
16 Tbs = 1 glass (or a standard measuring cup)

Apothecary Units

In the apothecary system

The unit of weight is the *grain.*
The unit of volume is the *minim.*

Of the many units of measure in the apothecary system, you should know the following units, abbreviations, and equivalents.

Weight

60 grains (gr) = 1 dram (dr or ʒ)
8 drams (dr or ʒ) = 1 ounce (oz or ʒ)

Volume

60 minims (min) = 1 fluid dram (fl dr or fʒ)
8 fl dr = 1 fluid ounce (fl oz or fʒ)
16 fl oz = 1 pint (pt)
2 pt = 1 quart (qt)
4 qt = 1 gallon (gal)

In the apothecary system, when the symbol or abbreviation is used, the quantity is written in lowercase Roman numerals and

TABLE 2-1 Equivalents and Conversions (Continued)
••

follows the symbol. Arabic numerals are used, however, in preference to large Roman numerals. For example

5 gr = gr v
8 dr = ʒ viii
The quantity one-half may be indicated by the symbol ss.
1½ gr = gr iss
7½ gr = gr viiss

Other fractional parts are expressed as common fractions, for example, gr ¹⁄₂₅₀, gr ¹⁄₁₀.
When pint, quart, and gallon are written, the quantity is expressed in Arabic numerals (eg, 1½ pints or 7½ quarts).

Apothecary Units and Their Household Equivalents

1 drop = 1 minim (m i)
1 tsp = 1 dr (ʒ i)
1 Tbs = 1/2 oz (ʒ ss)
2 Tbs = 1 oz (ʒ i)
1 teacup = 6 oz (ʒ vi)
1 glass or measuring cup = 8 oz (ʒ viii)
2 measuring cups = 1 pt

MOST COMMONLY USED APPROXIMATE EQUIVALENTS*

Metric	Apothecary	Household
0.06 g	gr i	
0.06 mL	min i	1 drop
1.0 g	gr xv	
1.0 mL	min xv	⅕ tsp
5 mL	(1 dr) ʒ i	1 tsp
15 mL	(½ oz) ʒ ss	1 Tbs
30 mL	(1 oz) ʒ i	2 Tbs
500 mL	(16 oz) ʒ 16	1 pt
1000 mL	(32 oz) ʒ 32	1 qt

••

* There are many discrepancies among these approximate equivalents. For example, 30 mL is the accepted equivalent for 1 oz (29.57 mL is the exact equivalent); however, multiplying 5 mL per dram by 8 (ʒ viii per ounce) results in an equivalent of 40 mL for 1 oz rather than the accepted equivalent of 30 mL = 1 oz.

Such discrepancies are inevitable when two systems are used whose equivalents are not exact. The discrepancies are within a 10% margin of error, which usually is acceptable in pharmacology.

(continued)

TABLE 2-1 Equivalents and Conversions (Continued)

••

COMMONLY USED METRIC UNITS AND THEIR APPROXIMATE APOTHECARY EQUIVALENTS

Metric		Apothecary
1 g	1000 mg	gr xv
0.6 g	600 mg	gr x
0.5 g	500 mg	gr viiss
0.3 g	300 mg	gr v
0.2 g	200 mg	gr iii
0.1 g	100 mg	gr iss
0.06 g	60 mg	gr i
0.05 g	50 mg	gr $3/4$
0.03 g	30 mg	gr $1/2$ or gr ss
0.02 g	20 mg	gr $1/3$
0.016 g	16 mg	gr $1/4$
0.015 g	15 mg	gr $1/4$
0.010 g	10 mg	gr $1/6$
0.008 g	8 mg	gr $1/8$
0.006 g	6 mg	gr $1/10$
0.005 g	5 mg	gr $1/12$
0.003 g	3 mg	gr $1/20$
0.002 g	2 mg	gr $1/30$
0.001 g	1 mg	gr $1/60$
	0.6 mg	gr $1/100$
	0.5 mg	gr $1/120$
	0.4 mg	gr $1/150$
	0.3 mg	gr $1/200$

••

TABLE 2-2 Body Surface Nomogram

••

Height	Surface Area (m²)	Weight

Feet and Inches	cm		lb	kg

```
                                                   440 ═══   200
                                                   420 ═══   190
                                                   400 ═══   180
                                                   380 ═══   170
                                                   360 ═══   160
                                                   340 ═══   150
                    220          3.00              320 ═══   140
              7'    215          2.90              300 ═══
              10"   210          2.80              290 ═══   130
              8"    205          2.70              280 ═══
              6"    200          2.60              270 ═══   120
              4"    195        ·· 2.50             260 ═══
              2"    190          2.40              250 ═══   110
              6'    185          2.30              240 ═══
              10"   180          2.20              230 ═══
              8"    175          2.10              220 ═══   100
              6"    170          2.00              210 ═══   95
              4"    165          1.95              200 ═══   90
              2"    160          1.90              190 ═══   85
              5'    155          1.85              180 ═══   80
                    150          1.80              170 ═══   75
              10"   145          1.75              160 ═══   70
              8"    140          1.70              150 ═══
              6"    135          1.65              140 ═══   65
              4"    130          1.60              130 ═══   60
              2"    125          1.55              120 ═══   55
              4'    120          1.50              110 ═══   50
              10"   115          1.45              100 ═══   45
              8"    110          1.40               90 ═══   40
              6"    105          1.35               80 ═══   35
              4"    100          1.30               70 ═══   30
              2"     95          1.25               60 ═══   25
              3'     90          1.20               50 ═══   20
              10"    85          1.15
              8"     80          1.10
              6"     75          1.05
```

To determine the surface area of the patient, draw a straight line from the point representing the patient's height on the left vertical scale to the point representing the patient's weight on the right vertical scale. The point at which this line intersects the middle vertical scale represents the surface area in square meters. (Courtesy of Abbott Laboratories.)

TABLE 2-3 Pediatric Body Surface Nomogram

Height	Surface Area (m²)	Weight

Feet and Inches	cm		lb	kg

To determine the surface area of the patient, draw a straight line from the point representing the patient's height on the left vertical scale to the point representing the patient's weight on the right vertical scale. The point at which this line intersects the middle vertical scale represents the surface area in square meters. (Courtesy of Abbott Laboratories.)

TABLE 2-4 DEA Schedules of Controlled Substances
••

The Controlled Substances Act of 1970 regulates the manufacturing, distribution, and dispensing of drugs that are known to have abuse potential. The Drug Enforcement Agency (DEA) is responsible for the enforcement of these regulations. The controlled drugs are divided into five DEA schedules based on their potential for abuse and physical and psychological dependence.

Schedule I (*C-I*): High abuse potential and no accepted medical use (heroin, marijuana, LSD)

Schedule II (*C-II*): High abuse potential with severe dependence liability (narcotics, amphetamines, and barbiturates)

Schedule III (*C-III*): Less abuse potential than Schedule II drugs and moderate dependence liability (nonbarbiturate sedatives, nonamphetamine stimulants, limited amounts of certain narcotics)

Schedule IV (*C-IV*): Less abuse potential than Schedule III and limited dependence liability (some sedatives, antianxiety agents, and nonnarcotic analgesics)

Schedule V (*C-V*): Limited abuse potential. Primarily small amounts of narcotics (codeine) used as antitussives or antidiarrheals. Under federal law, limited quantities of certain Schedule V drugs may be purchased without a prescription directly from a pharmacist. The purchaser must be at least 18 years of age and must furnish suitable identification. All such transactions must be recorded by the dispensing pharmacist.

Prescribing physicians and dispensing pharmacists must be registered with the DEA, which also provides forms for the transfer of Schedule I and II substances and establishes criteria for the inventory and prescribing of controlled substances. State and local laws are often more stringent than federal law. In any given situation, the more stringent law applies.
••

TABLE 2-5 FDA Pregnancy Categories

The Food and Drug Administration has established five categories to indicate the potential for a systemically absorbed drug to cause birth defects. The key differentiation among the categories rests upon the degree (reliability) of documentation and the risk-benefit ratio.

Category A: Adequate studies in pregnant women have not demonstrated a risk to the fetus in the first trimester of pregnancy, and there is no evidence of risk in later trimesters.

Category B: Animal studies have not demonstrated a risk to the fetus but there are no adequate studies in pregnant women. *or* Animal studies have shown an adverse effect, but adequate studies in pregnant women have not demonstrated a risk to the fetus during the first trimester of pregnancy, and there is no evidence of risk in later trimesters.

Category C: Animal studies have shown an adverse effect on the fetus but there are no adequate studies in humans; the benefits from the use of the drug in pregnant women may be acceptable despite its potential risks. *or* There are no animal reproduction studies and no adequate studies in humans.

Category D: There is evidence of human fetal risk, but the potential benefits from the use of the drug in pregnant women may be acceptable despite its potential risks.

Category X: Studies in animals or humans demonstrate fetal abnormalities or adverse reaction; reports indicate evidence of fetal risk. The risk of use in a pregnant woman clearly outweighs any possible benefit.

Regardless of the designated Pregnancy Category or presumed safety, *no* drug should be administered during pregnancy unless it is clearly needed.

TABLE 2-6 Narcotic Equianalgesic Dosages
••

The following are dosages for equal relief of pain when used in the acute care setting for the narcotic drugs below. Chronic administration or abuse of these drugs may alter the pharmacokinetics of the drugs, resulting in varying equivalents.

Drug	Duration	Half-life	Route	Equianalgesic Dosage
Buprenorphine	4–6 h	2–3 h	IM	0.4 mg
			PO	0.8 mg
Butorphanol	3–4 h	2.5–3.5 h	IM	2 mg
Codeine	4–6 h	3 h	IM	120 mg
			PO	200 mg
Dezocine	3–6 h	2.4 h	IM	10 mg
Fentanyl	1–2 h	1.5–6 h	IM	0.1 mg
			PO	NA
Hydrocodone	4–8 h	3.3–4.5 h	NA	NA
Levorphanol	6–8 h	12–16 h	IM	2 mg
			PO	4 mg
Meperidine	2–4 h	3–4 h	IM	75 mg
			PO	300 mg
Methadone	4–6 h	15–30 h	IM	10 mg
			PO	20 mg
Morphine	3–7 h	1.5–2 h	IM	10 mg
			PO	60 mg
Nalbuphine	4–6 h	5 h	IM	10 mg
Oxycodone	4–6 h	NA	PO	30 mg
Oxymorphone	3–6 h	NA	IM	1 mg
			PO	10 mg
Pentazocine	4–7 h	2–3 h	IM	60 mg
			PO	180 mg
Propoxyphene	4–6 h	6–12 h	PO	130/200 mg
Sufentanil	NA	2.5 h	IM	0.02 mg

••

TABLE 2-7 Needle and Syringe Specifications

Type	Needle Gauge	Needle Length	Syringe	Comments
Intradermal	26	3/8 in	Tuberculin	Area must be marked or mapped if repeated tests done.
Subcutaneous	25	1/2 in	Tuberculin, insulin	Rotate sites.
Intramuscular	20–23	1–3 in	2–3 mL	Rapid insertion and slow injection help to decrease pain.
Intravenous	20, 21		Bag with tubing	Monitor site and needle placement.
Blood	16, 18		Bag with tubing	Check equipment, needle placement, and injection site regularly.

SUBCUTANEOUS SITES

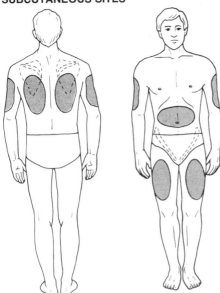

DORSOGLUTEAL SITE

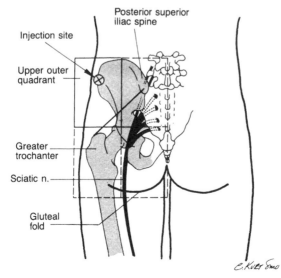

FIGURE 2-1 Injection sites. *(continued)*

VENTROGLUTEAL SITE

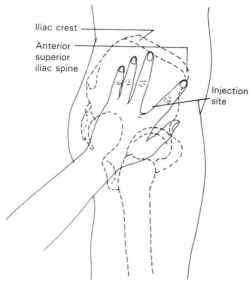

DELTOID SITE

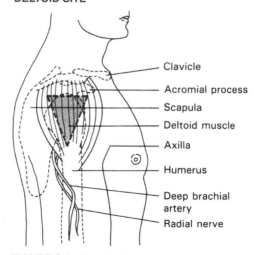

FIGURE 2-1 (Continued)

VASTUS LATERALIS SITE

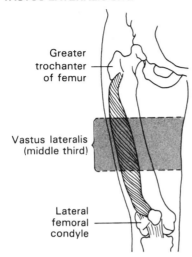

Greater trochanter of femur

Vastus lateralis (middle third)

Lateral femoral condyle

RECTUS FEMORIS SITE

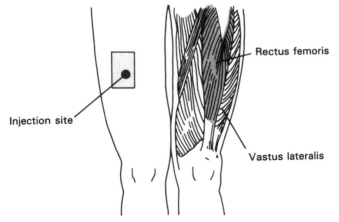

Injection site

Rectus femoris

Vastus lateralis

FIGURE 2-1 (Continued)

TABLE 2-8 Compatibility of Drugs in Syringe

	atropine	butorphanol	chlorpromazine	cimetidine	dimenhydrinate	dimenhydramine	fentanyl	glycopyrrolate	heparin
thiopental			N		N	N		N	
secobarbital				N				N	
ranitidine	Y		Y		Y	Y	Y	Y	
promethazine	M	Y	M	Y	N	M	M	Y	N
prochlorperazine	M	Y	Y	Y	N	M	M	Y	
pentobarbital	M	N	N	N	N	N	N	N	
pentazocine	M	Y	M	Y	M	M	M	N	N
nalbuphine	Y			Y					
morphine	M	Y	M	Y	M	M	M	Y	N
midazolam	Y	Y	Y	Y	N	Y	Y	Y	
metoclopramide	M		M		M	Y	M		M
meperidine	Y	M	M	Y	M	M	M	Y	N
hydroxyzine	Y	Y	M	Y	N	M	Y	Y	
heparin	M		N	Y	M		M		Y
glycopyrrolate	Y		Y	Y	N	Y			
fentanyl	M	Y	M	Y	M		Y		M
dimenhydramine	M	Y	M	Y	M	Y	M	Y	
dimenhydrinate	M	N	N		Y	M	M	N	M
cimetidine	Y	Y	N	Y			Y		Y
chlorpromazine	Y	Y	Y	N	N		M	Y	N
butorphanol	Y	Y	Y	Y	N	Y	Y		
atropine	Y	Y	Y	Y	M	M	M	Y	M

hydroxyzine	Y	Y	M	Y	N	M	Y	M	Y	Y	Y	M	Y	N	M	N	
meperidine	Y	M	M	N	M	M	Y	N	M	Y	M	Y	M	Y	Y	Y	N
metoclopramide	M		M		M		M	N	Y	M	M	Y	M	Y	M	Y	
midazolam	Y	Y	Y	N	Y		Y	N	Y	Y	Y	N	Y	N	N	Y	
morphine	M	M	M	M	M		M	M	Y	Y	M	M	M	Y	M	Y	N
nalbuphine	Y		Y			Y				Y				Y	Y		
pentazocine	M	Y	M	M	M	Y	M	N	Y	Y	M	Y	M	Y	Y	Y	
pentobarbital	M	N	N	N	N		N	N	N	N	N	N	N	Y	N		Y
prochlorperazine	M	Y	Y	M	M		Y	N	M	Y	M	Y	M	N	Y	Y	N
promethazine	M	Y	M	M	M	Y	M	N	Y	Y	M	Y	M	N	Y	Y	N
ranitidine	Y		Y	Y	Y	Y	Y	Y	Y	Y	Y	Y	Y		Y		
secobarbital		N														Y	
thiopental		N	N	N	N		N	N	N	Y	N	N	N	Y	N		Y

Key: Y = Compatible in syringe; M = Moderately compatible, inject immediately after combining; N = Incompatible, do not mix in syringe; Blank space = Information about compatibility is not currently available.

45

TABLE 2-9 Drug Compatibility Guide

	aminophylline	amphotericin B	ampicillin	atropine	calcium gluconate	carbenicillin	cefazolin	cimetidine	clindamycin	diazepam	dopamine	epinephrine	erythromycin	fentanyl	furosemide	gentamicin	glycopyrrolate	heparin sodium	hydrocortisone	hydroxyzine	levarterenol	lidocaine	meperidine	morphine	nitroglycerin	pentobarbital	potassium chloride	sodium bicarbonate	tetracycline	vancomycin	verapamil	vitamin B & C complex
aminophylline	•		Y		Y	N	N	N	N	Y	Y	N	N					Y	Y	N	N	Y	N	N	Y	Y	Y	Y	N	N	Y	N
amphotericin B		•	N		N	N		N			N					N		Y	Y			N					N	Y	N		N	
ampicillin	Y	N	•	N	N	Y	Y		N	N	N		N			N	Y	Y	N			Y					Y	Y	N		Y	Y
atropine			N	•			Y	Y					Y	Y				N		Y	N		Y	Y		N	Y				Y	
calcium gluconate	Y	N	N		•		N		N	Y	Y	N	Y					Y	Y		Y	Y					Y	N	N	Y	Y	Y
carbenicillin	N	N	Y			•		Y	Y	N	Y	N	N			N			Y		N	Y					Y	N	N		Y	Y
cefazolin	N			N			•	N		N			N			N			Y		N	N				N	Y		N		Y	Y
cimetidine	N	N	Y	Y		Y	N	•	Y				Y		Y	Y		Y			Y	Y				N	Y		Y	Y	Y	N
clindamycin	Y	Y				Y	N		•							Y		Y	Y							N	Y				Y	Y
diazepam	Y	Y			Y	N	N		N	•		N			N		N	N		N	N	N	N	N		N	N	Y			Y	Y
dopamine	Y	Y			N	Y				N	•					N		Y	Y			Y			Y		Y	N			Y	Y
epinephrine	N	Y				N		Y				•	N		N			Y			N	N	Y				N				Y	N
erythromycin	Y	Y	Y	Y	N	Y	N	Y				N	•					Y	Y			Y				N	Y	N	Y	Y	Y	Y
fentanyl					Y		N		Y	Y			Y	•	N			N		Y			Y	Y		N						
furosemide	Y	Y		N		Y		Y				N			•	N		Y			N				Y		Y		N		Y	Y

																									Y	Y
gentamicin			N	N			N	N			Y		N	N			Y			N				N			Y	Y
glycopyrrolate	N	N		Y						N		•		N													
heparin sodium	Y	Y	Y	N	Y	Y	N	N	N	Y	Y	•	N	Y	Y	Y	N	N	Y	Y	N	Y	N	N	Y	Y	Y
hydrocortisone	Y	Y	N		N	Y		Y	Y		•	N	•	Y		Y	Y		Y	Y	Y				Y	Y	Y
hydroxyzine	N			Y		N			Y	Y	•	N	Y														N
levarterenol	N	Y	N	N	Y		N	N		Y	Y	•	Y	N		N	Y		Y		Y		N	Y		Y	Y
lidocaine	Y	N	Y	Y	N	Y	Y	Y	Y	Y	Y	•	Y	Y	Y	Y	Y		Y	Y	Y	Y	Y	Y	Y	Y	Y
meperidine	N		Y	N		Z	Y		Y	Y	•	N	N	Z		N	N	•	Y		N	N	N	N'		Y	Y
morphine	N		Y	N		Y	Y	Y	•	N	N	Y	N		Y	Y	Y		N	Y	Y			Y	N	Y	Y
nitroglycerin	Y				Y					Y		•		Y		Y	•		Y							Y	
pentobarbital	Y		N	N		N	N	N	N		N		Z	N		N	N	•	N	N	Y	N	N	N	N	N	Y
potassium chloride	Y	N	Y	Y	Y	Y	Y	N	Y	Y	Y	Y	Y	Y	•	Y	Y	Y	Y	Y	Y	Y	•	Y	Y	Y	Y
sodium bicarbonate	Y	Y	N	N	N	N	Y	Y	Y		Y	Y		Y	•	Y	N	N	Y	Y	N	N	N	•	N	N	N
tetracycline	N	N	N	N		Y		N	N	Z	N	Y	Y		N	Y	N		N	Y	N	Y		•			Y
vancomycin	N	Y	Y	Y		N	Y	N	Y		Y	Y	Y		Y	Y	N		N	Y	N	N	•			Y	Y
verapamil	Y	Y	Y	Y	Y	Y	Y	Y	Y	Y	Y	Y	Y	Y	Y	Y	Y	Y	Y	Y	Y	Y	Y	Y	•	Y	Y
vitamin B & C complex	N	N	Y	Y		Y	N	N	Y	Y	N	Y	N	Y	Y	Y	Y		Y	N	Y	N	Y	Y	Y	•	

Key: Y = Compatible; N = Incompatible; Blank space = Information about compatibility was not available.

NOTE: Because the compatibility of two or more drugs in solution depends on several variables such as the solution itself, drug concentration, and the method of mixing (bottle, syringe, or Y-site), this table is intended to be used solely as a guide to general drug compatibilities. Before mixing any drugs, the health care professional should ascertain if a potential incompatibility exists by referring to an appropriate information source.

(Reprinted from Malseed RT, Goldstein FJ, Balkon N. *Pharmacology: Drug therapy and nursing management* [4th ed]. Philadelphia: JB Lippincott, 1995.)

TABLE 2-10 Composition of Selected IV Solutions

Solution	Tonicity	Na⁺	K⁺	Cl⁻	Ca⁺⁺	pH	mOsm/L	Calories
		\multicolumn{4}{c}{(mEq/L)}			
5% DW	Isotonic	—	—	—	—	5.0	253	170
10% DW	Hypertonic	—	—	—	—	4.6	561	340
0.9% NS	Isotonic	154	—	154	—	5.7	308	—
0.45% NS	Hypotonic	77	—	77	—	5.3	154	—
5% D and 0.9% NS*	Slightly hypertonic	154	—	154	—	4.2	561	170
5% and 0.45% NS	Slightly hypertonic	77	—	77	—	4.2	407	170
5% and 0.2% NS	Hypotonic	34	—	34	—	4.2	290	170
Lactated Ringer's†	Isotonic	148	4	156	4.5	6.7	309	9
5% D and lactated Ringer's	Slightly hypertonic	130	4	109	3.0	5.1	527	170
Normosol-R	Isotonic	140	5	96	—	6.4	295	—
Sodium lactate 1/6 molar	Slightly hypertonic	167	—	—	—	6.9	333	55
6% Dextran 75 and 0.9% NS	Isotonic	154	—	154	—	4.3	309	—

DW, dextrose in water; NS, normal saline

* 5% dextrose metabolizes rapidly in the blood and, in reality, produces minimal osmotic effects.

† Lactate converts to bicarbonate in the liver.

48

TABLE 2-11 Flow Rates for IV Infusions

$$\frac{\text{Total fluid volume}}{\text{Total time (minutes)}} \times \text{Drop factor (drops/mL)} = \text{Infusion rate (drops/min)}$$

Drop Factor of Tubing (drops/mL)	1000 mL/6 h (drops/min)	1000 mL/8 h (drops/min)
10	28	21
15	42	31
20	56	42
60	167	125

1000 mL/10 h (drops/min)	1000 mL/12 h (drops/min)	1000 mL/24 h (drops/min)
17	14	7
25	21	10
34	28	14
100	84	42

TABLE 2-12 IV Catheter Maintenance Guidelines

Catheter	Dressing Change	Flush (Maintenance)	Flush (After Blood Draw)
Short peripheral	3d when site changed	If used as a lock, 2 mL saline every shift or heparin 1:10 units/mL	N/A
Midline (ie, Landmark)	q 3–5d	3 mL 1:10 units/mL heparin qd	5 mL normal saline 3 mL 1:100 units/mL heparin
PICC	3 times/wk postinsertion, weekly after that	2–3 mL 1:100 units/mL heparin qd	10 mL normal saline 3 mL 1:10 units/mL heparin
Groshong	q 1–2d postinsertion for a week postop, then q 3d until site fully healed, then every week. When site healed, no dressing. Secure catheter to chest with tape.	10 mL normal saline weekly	10 mL normal saline

Catheter	Dressing/care	Flush protocol	Declotting/amounts
Hickman/Broviac	Same as Groshong	3 mL 1:100 units qd. If accessed q 8h or more frequently, no need for heparin between infusions.	10 mL normal saline 3 mL 1:100 units/mL heparin
Implanted ports (including PAS Port)	Needle and dressing change every week when accessed	If accessed and locked: 5 mL normal saline and 5 mL 1:100 units/mL heparin after each infusion. Terminal flush: 5–7 mL 1:100 units/mL heparin and q 4wk thereafter	5 mL normal saline 5 mL 1:100 units/mL heparin
Percutaneous catheters (triple/double lumen)	q 2–3d	3 mL normal saline 2 mL 1:10 units heparin twice per day or after each infusion	3 mL normal saline 3 mL 1:10 units heparin
Quinton/Perm-A catheter (blue lumen, use only with order)	q 2–3d	3 mL normal saline 2 mL 1000 units/mL heparin q 2–3d (always withdraw heparin first when using catheter)	10 mL normal saline 2 mL 1000 units/mL heparin

TABLE 2-13 Patient Teaching Guide

••

Patient's name _____

Prescriber's name _____

Phone number _____

Instructions:

1. The name of your drug is _____.
2. The dose of the drug that is ordered for you is
   _____.
3. Special storage instruction for your drug:

4. The drug should be taken _____ times a day. The best
   time to take your drug is _____ , _____ , etc.
5. The drug should (not) be taken with meals, because food
   will affect the way the drug is absorbed.
6. Special activities that should be considered when taking
   this drug:

7. Be aware that the following side effects may occur:

8. Do not take this drug with other drugs, including over-the-
   counter medications, without first checking with your
   health care provider.
9. Tell any nurse, physician, or dentist who is taking care of
   you that you are taking this drug.
10. Keep this and all medications out of the reach of children.

Notify your nurse or physician if any of the following occur:

1. Report: (specific signs or symptoms associated with drug
   toxicity)

2. Abrupt stoppage of the drug. Abrupt stoppage of this drug
   can cause _____ .

TABLE 2-13 Patient Teaching Guide (Continued)

Whenever a patient is given the responsibility for drug administration, there are certain facts to which the patient should have ready access. Some states require that patients be given written information about their drugs. Nursing care always includes patient teaching activities. This teaching guide is designed to be copied for distribution to the patient, and the specific information about each drug—which is found in the patient teaching section of each drug monograph—can be added for a quick, precise teaching aid. The patient needs to know what the drug is and the dosage prescribed, especially if he or she sees more than one physician or travels; special storage information; how many times a day and *when* the drug should be taken; how to take the drug in relation to meals; specific adverse effects that are expected with this drug; special precautions or activities that are related to the use of this drug, including follow-up visits or tests; signs and symptoms to report to his or her health care provider; and dangers of abrupt stoppage of the drug. Good practice also requires reminding the patient to avoid all other medications (including OTC drugs) without first checking with his or her health care provider, to keep drugs away from children, and to report to any other health care provider that he or she is taking this drug.

TABLE 2-14 Blood Plasma Concentration of Commonly Monitored Drugs

Drug	Therapeutic* Maintenance	Toxic† (Panic or Critical)
Acetaminophen (Tylenol)	1–30 µg/mL or 66–199 µmol/L	>200 µg/mL or >1324 µmol/L
Alcohol (ethanol)	Driving while intoxicated: 100 mg/dL or 10.9–21.7 mmol/L	>400 mg/dL >86.8 mmol/L
Amitriptyline (Elavil)	120–250 mg/mL or 433–903 nmol/L	>500 mg/mL or >1805 nmol/L
Bromide	750–1500 µg/mL or 9.4–18.7 nmol/L	>1250 µg/mL or >15.6 nmol/L >15.6 nmol/L
Carbamazepine (Tegretol)	8–12 µg/mL or 34–51 µmol/L	>15 µg/mL or >63 mol/L

(continued)

TABLE 2-14 Blood Plasma Concentration of Commonly Monitored Drugs (Continued)

Drug	Therapeutic* Maintenance	Toxic† (Panic or Critical)
Chlordiazepoxide (Librium)	700–1000 ng/mL or 2.34–3.34 µmol/L	>5000 ng/mL or >16.70 µmol/L
Desopyramide (Norpace)	Variable	>7 µg/mL or >20.7 µmol/L
Diazepam (Valium)	100–1000 ng/mL or 0.35–3.51 µmol/L	>5000 ng/mL or >17.55 µmol/L
Digitoxin	20–35 ng/mL or 26–46 nmol/L	>45 ng/mL or >59 nmol/L
Digoxin	CHF: 0.8–1.5 ng/mL or 1.0–1.9 nmol/L Arrhythmias: 1.5–2.0 ng/mL or 1.9–2.6 nmol/L	>25 ng/mL or >3.2 nmol/L
Doxepin	30–150 ng/mL or 107–537 nmol/L	>500 ng/mL or >1790 nmol/L
Ethchlorvynol (Placidyl)	2–8 µg/mL or 14–55 µmol/L	>20 µg/mL or >138 µmol/L
Glutethimide (Doriden)	2–6 µg/mL or 9–28 µmol/L	>5 µg/mL or >23 µmol/L
Imipramine (Tofranil)	125–250 ng/mL or 446–893 nmol/L	>500 ng/mL or >1785 nmol/L
Lithium	0.6–1.2 mEq/L or 0.6–1.2 mmol/L	>2 mEq/L or >2 mmol/L
Lidocaine (Xylocaine)	1.5–6.0 µg/mL or 6.4–25.6 µmol/L	6–8 µg/mL or >25.6–34.2 µmol/L
Methotrexate	Variable	48 h after high dose: 454 mg/mL or 1000 mmol/L
Methyprylon (Noludar)	8–10 µg/mL or 45–55 µmol/L	>50 µg/mL or >275 µmol/L
Phenobarbital	15–40 g/mL or 65–172 mol/L	Varies: 35–80 g/mL or 151–345 mol/L
Phenytoin (Dilantin)	10–20 g/mL or 40–79 mol/L	Varies with symptoms
Procainamide (Promestyl)	4–10 g/mL or 17–42 mol/L	10–12 g/mL or 42–51 mol/L
Primidone (Mysoline)	5–12 g/mL or 23–35 mol/L	15 g/mL or 69 mol/L
Propranolol (Inderal)	50–100 mg/mL or 193–386 nmol/L	Not defined

TABLE 2-14 Blood Plasma Concentration of Commonly Monitored Drugs (Continued)

Drug	Therapeutic* Maintenance	Toxic† (Panic or Critical)
Salicylate	<100 µg/mL or <724 µmol/L	Quite variable: begins at 100 µg/mL or begins at 724 µmol/L
Theophylline	Bronchodilator: 8–20 µg/mL or 44–111 µmol/L Premature apnea: 6–13 µg/mL or 33–72 µmol/L	>20 µg/mL or >111 µmol/L
Valproic acid (Depakene)	50–100 g/mL or 347–693 µmol/L	100 g/mL or 693 µmol/L

* *Therapeutic value* refers to expected drug concentration associated with desirable clinical effects in majority of the patient population treated.

† *Toxic value* refers to the drug concentration associated with undesirable effects or, in certain cases, death.

TABLE 2-15 Blood Plasma Concentration of Commonly Monitored Antibiotics

Antibiotic	Peak*	Trough†
Amikacin	Therapeutic: 25–35 µg/mL or 43–600 µmol/L Toxic: >35 µg/mL or >6000 µmol/L	Less severe infections: 1–4 µg/mL Therapeutic: 1.71–6.84 µmol/L Toxic: >5 µg/mL or >17 µmol/L
Ethosuximide		Therapeutic: 40–100 µg/mL or 283–708 µmol/L Toxic: >150 µg/mL or >1062 µmol/L
Gentamicin	Less severe infection: Therapeutic: 5–8 µg/mL Toxic: >12 µg/mL	Less severe: Therapeutic: 1–4 µg/mL Toxic: >4 µg/mL
Kanamycin	Therapeutic: 8–25 µg/mL Toxic: >25 µg/mL	Therapeutic: 2–8 µg/mL Toxic: >8 µg/mL
Tobramycin	Less severe: Therapeutic: 5–9 µg/mL or 11–17 µmol/L Toxic: >12 µg/mL or 21–26 µmol/L	Less severe: 1–3 µg/mL Therapeutic: <2 µmol/L Toxic: >3 µg/mL or >4–9 µmol/L

* *Peak drug level* refers to maximum drug concentration achieved following administration of a single dose. For a specific drug, both the concentration achieved and the time interval between dosing and peak drug level required may vary considerably from patient to patient.

† *Trough drug level* refers to minimum drug concentration preceding administration of a single dose.

CHAPTER 3

Respiratory
Reference Facts

TABLE 3-1 Types of Respirations

	Description	Pattern
Normal	12–20/min and regular	∿∿∿
Apnea	Absence of respiration	────
Bradypnea	<12/min and regular	∿⌒
Tachypnea	>20/min and regular	∿∿∿∿∿
Hyperventilation	Increased rate and increased depth	ΛΛΛΛ
Hypoventilation	Decreased rate and decreased depth	──∿──
Cheyne-Stokes	Periods of apnea and hyperventilation	ΛΛ__ΛΛ
Kussmaul	Very deep with normal rhythm	ΛΛΛΛ

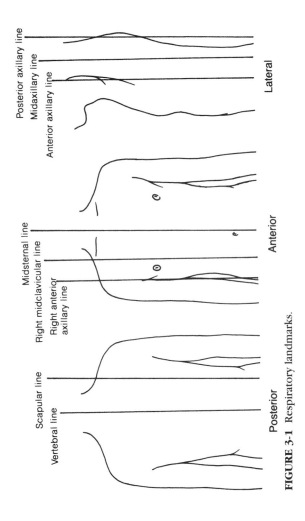

FIGURE 3-1 Respiratory landmarks.

60

NORMAL BREATH SOUNDS

BRONCHIAL OR TUBULAR

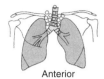

Anterior

Ratio of Inspiration to Expiration

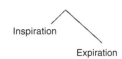

Inspiration

Expiration

Blowing, hollow sounds auscultated over the trachea

Inspiration is shorter than expiration. Expiration is longer, lower and higher-pitched than inspiration

BRONCHOVESICULAR

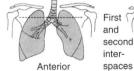

First and second interspaces

Anterior   Posterior

Scapula

Inspiration   Expiration

Medium-pitched, medium intensity, blowing sounds auscultated over the first and second interspaces anteriorly and the scapula posteriorly

Inspiration and expiration have similar pitch

VESICULAR

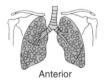

Anterior   Posterior

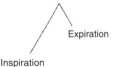

Expiration

Inspiration

Soft, low-pitched sounds auscultated over the lung periphery

Inspiration is longer, louder, and higher-pitched than expiration

FIGURE 3-2 Normal and abnormal breath sounds. *(continued)*

ABNORMAL BREATH SOUNDS

BREATH SOUNDS   CHARACTERISTICS

Wheeze

Musical or squeaking
High- pitched and continuous sounds
Auscultated during inspiration or expiration
Occurs in small air passages

Rhonchi

Sonorous or coarse
Low-pitched and continuous sounds
Auscultated during inspiration and expiration
Occurs in large air passages
(Coughing may clear the sound)

Crackles

Bubbling, crackling, popping
Low- to high-pitched, discontinuous sounds
Auscultated during inspiration
Occurs in small air passages, alveoli,
     bronchioles, bronchi, and trachea

Friction rub

Rubbing or grating
Loudest over lower lateral anterior surface
Auscultated during inspiration and expiration

FIGURE 3-2   (Continued)

TABLE 3-2   Oxygen Administration Devices

Device	Oxygen Capability	Nursing Considerations
Cannula (nasal prongs)	22%–44% when operated at 1–6 L/min	1. Most commonly used oxygen device because of convenience and client comfort 2. Delivered oxygen concentration can vary with client breathing pattern. "Rule of Four" used to estimate concentration: for each L/min of O_2, concentration increases by 4% (eg, 1 L/min provides 22%, 2 L/min provides 26%)

TABLE 3-2 Oxygen Administration
Devices (Continued)

● ●

Device	Oxygen Capability	Nursing Considerations
		3. Limit maximum O_2 flow to 6 L/min to minimize drying of nasal mucosa; use humidifier prn
		4. Nasal passages must be patent for client to receive O_2; mouth breathing does not appreciably diminish delivered O_2
		5. Delivered O_2 concentration can vary, depending on client's breathing pattern. Relatively consistent O_2 delivery with quiet, steady breathing
Transtracheal catheter	0.5–2 L/min	1. Device is surgically implanted in trachea of O_2-dependent client as alternative to cannula
		2. Advantages: efficient use of O_2 (no waste, because all O_2 is delivered directly to lungs); practically invisible so client feels less self-conscious
		3. Suitable only for clients who can care for device
Venturi mask	24%–50% when operated at 3–8 L/min as specified by manufacturer	1. Provides precise and consistent O_2 concentration
		2. Essential to adjust mask according to specifications to ensure accurate O_2 delivery
		3. Noisy; like all masks may cause claustrophobia
Simple mask	40%–60% when operated at 6–10 L/min	1. Most common midrange O_2 delivery device
		2. Minimum of 5 L/min O_2 required to prevent client

(continued)

TABLE 3-2 Oxygen Administration Devices (Continued)

Device	Oxygen Capability	Nursing Considerations
Simple mask *(cont.)*		from rebreathing exhaled carbon dioxide 3. As with cannula, actual delivered O_2 concentration varies with breathing pattern 4. Not suitable for client with COPD because of potential for excessive oxygenation
Reservoir mask	Up to 90%+ when operated at 10–15 L/min	1. Used for critically ill client 2. Use sufficient flow to keep O_2 reservoir inflated
Large volume pneumatic nebulizer	21%–100% when operated at 12–15 L/min	1. Used to deliver O_2 with continuous aerosol therapy; required by many clients with artificial airways (eg, tracheostomies) 2. Temperature must be monitored and tubing must be drained frequently
Incubator	22%–40%+	1. Enclosure used for environmental control for newborn infants 2. Extremely imprecise O_2 delivery: accuracy varies each time unit is opened
Oxyhood	22%–90%+ when operated at 7–12 L/min	1. Precise O_2 delivery for newborns and small infants 2. Minimum O_2 flow of 7 L/min flushes infant's exhaled carbon dioxide 3. Oxygen must be prewarmed and humidified

TABLE 3-2 Oxygen Administration
Devices (Continued)

Device	Oxygen Capability	Nursing Considerations
		to prevent infant heat loss
		4. Frequent analysis needed to prevent excessive oxygenation
Oxygen tent	21%–30%+	1. Primarily used by small child unable to wear mask or cannula
		2. Mainly used as "mist tent" to deliver high humidity to children with croup
		3. Extremely inefficient O_2 delivery system; O_2 delivery fluctuates because leaks are common

COPD, chronic obstructive pulmonary disease.

TABLE 3-3 Approximate Oxygen Concentrations

••

Because a nasal cannula is a low-flow system (patient's tidal volume supplies part of the inspired gas), oxygen concentration will vary, depending on the patient's respiratory rate and tidal volume. Approximate oxygen concentrations delivered are:

    1 L = 24% to 25%
    2 L = 27% to 29%
    3 L = 30% to 33%
    4 L = 33% to 37%
    5 L = 36% to 41%
    6 L = 39% to 45%

••

TABLE 3-4 Normal Arterial Blood Gas Values

••

	Arterial Blood	Mixed Venous Blood
pH	7.40 (7.35–7.45)	7.38 (7.33–7.43)
Po_2	80–100 mm Hg	35–49 mm Hg
O_2 sat	95% or greater	70%–75%
Pco_2	35–45 mm Hg	41–51 mm Hg
Hco_3^-	22–26 mEq/L	24–28 mEq/L
Base excess (BE)	−2 to +2	0 to +4

••

TABLE 3-5 Changes in Arterial Blood Gas Values with Respiratory Acid–Base Imbalances

Imbalance	pH	Paco$_2$	Hco$_3$	Base Excess
ACIDOSIS				
Uncompensated respiratory acidosis (acute)	↓	↑	N	N
Partially compensated respiratory acidosis	↓	↑	↑	↑
Completely compensated respiratory acidosis	N	↑	↑	↑
ALKALOSIS				
Uncompensated respiratory alkalosis	↑	↓	N	N
Partially compensated respiratory alkalosis	↑	↓	↓	↓
Completely compensated respiratory alkalosis	N	↓	↓	↓

N, normal.

TABLE 3-6 Endotracheal Tube Sizes

Patient	ET Tube Size	Suction Catheter
Adult female	7.0 mm	10 F
	8.0 mm	12 F
	8.5 mm	14 F
Adult male	8.5 mm	14 F
	9.0 mm	16 F
	10.0 mm	18 F

F, French.

TABLE 3-7 Pulmonary Function Tests

Term	Symbol	Description	Remarks
Vital capacity	VC	Maximum volume of air exhaled after a maximum inspiration	VC < 10–15 mL/kg suggests need for mechanical ventilation VC > 10–15 mL/kg suggests ability to wean
Forced vital capacity	FVC	Vital capacity performed with a maximally forced expiratory effort	Reduced in obstructive disease (COPD) due to air trapping Reflects airflow in large airways
Forced expiratory volume in 1 second	FEV_1	Volume of air exhaled in the first second of the performance of a FVC	Reduced in obstructive disease (COPD) due to air trapping Reflects airflow in larger airways
Ratio of FEV_1/FVC	FEV_1/FVC	FEV_1 expressed as a percentage of the FVC	Decreased in obstructive disease Normal in restrictive disease
Forced midexpiratory flow	$FEF_{25\%-75\%}$	Average flow during the middle half of the FVC	Reflects airflow in small airways Smokers may have change in this test before other symptoms develop
Peak expiratory flow rate	PEFR	Most rapid flow during a forced expiration after a maximum inspiration	Used to measure response to bronchodilators, airflow obstruction in patients with asthma
Maximal voluntary ventilation	MVV	Volume of air expired in a specified period (usually 10 to 15 seconds) during repetitive maximal effort	An important factor in exercise tolerance

CHAPTER 4

Cardiovascular Reference Facts

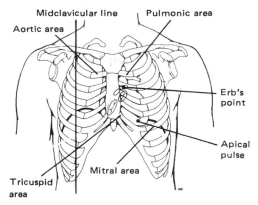

FIGURE 4-1 Cardiac landmarks.

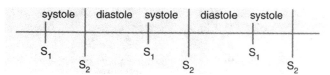

FIGURE 4-2 Normal heart sounds.

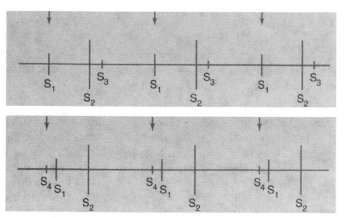

FIGURE 4-3 Abnormal heart sounds.

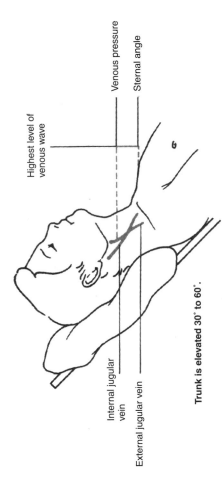

Highest level of
venous wave

Venous pressure

Sternal angle

Internal jugular
vein

External jugular vein

Trunk is elevated 30° to 60°.

FIGURE 4-4 Jugular venous distention assessment.

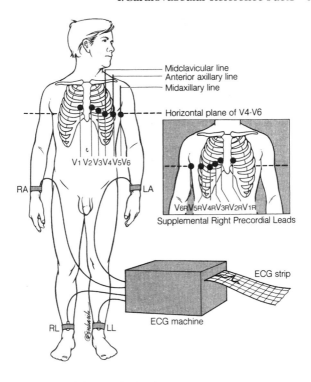

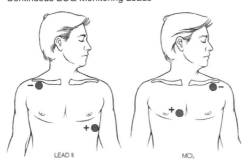

FIGURE 4-5 ECG lead placement.

TABLE 4-1 Hemodynamic Assessment of Myocardial Infarction

Pulmonary Capillary Wedge Pressure (mm Hg)	Cardiac Index (L/min/m^2)	Clinical State	Anticipated Therapy
<18	>2.2	Normal	Reduced metabolic needs
<18	<2.2	Volume depletion	Volume expansion with crystalloids
>18	>2.2	Pulmonary congestion	Diuretics Nitrates
>18	<2.2	Cardiogenic shock	Vasopressors Inotropic agents Afterload reducers IABP

IABP, intra-aortic balloon pump.

TABLE 4-2 Cardiac Enzymes after Acute Myocardial Infarction

	Increase	Peak	Return to Normal
CK	3–8 h	10–30 h	2–3 d
CK-MB	3–6 h	10–24 h	2–3 d
CK-MB$_2$	1–6 h	4–8 h	12–48 h
LDH	14–24 h	48–72 h	7–14 d
LDH$_1$	14–24 h	48–72 h	7–14 d

TABLE 4-3 Common Grading Systems for Heart Murmurs

••

INTENSITY

Grade I–Very faint, heard only after the listener has "tuned in"; may not be heard in all positions
Grade 2–Quiet but heard immediately upon placing the stethoscope on the chest
Grade 3–Moderately loud
Grade 4–Loud
Grade 5–Very loud, may be heard with a stethoscope partly off the chest
Grade 6–May be heard with the stethoscope entirely off the chest

⎫
⎬ Thrills are associated
⎭

PITCH

High, medium, or low

QUALITY

Blowing, rumbling, harsh, or musical

••

(Adapted from Bates B: A Guide to Physical Examination and History Taking, 5th ed. Philadelphia, JB Lippincott, 1991.)

TABLE 4-4 Lipoprotein Tests

••

CHOLESTEROL

Normal Values

Normal values vary with age, diet, and geographic or cultural region.
Adults: *Desirable level:* 140–199 mg/dL, or <5.18 mmol/L
           Borderline high: 200–239 mg/dL, or 5.18–6.19 mmol/L
           High: 240 mg/dL or higher, or >6.20 mmol/L
Children and adolescents (age 12–18):
           Desirable level: <170 mg/dL, or <4.39 mmol/L
           Borderline: 170–199 mg/dL, or 4.40–5.16 mmol/L
           High: >200 mg/dL, or >5.18 mmol/L

(continued)

TABLE 4-4 Lipoprotein Tests (Continued)
••

HIGH-DENSITY LIPOPROTEIN CHOLESTEROL (HDL-C)

Normal Values

Male: 37–70 mg/dL
Female: 40–85 mg/dL

<25 mg/dL of HDL	CHD risk is at dangerous level
26–35 mg/dL of HDL	High CHD risk
36–44 mg/dL of HDL	Moderate CHD risk
45–59 mg/dL of HDL	Average CHD risk
60–74 mg/dL of HDL	Below average CHD risk
>75 mg/dL of HDL	Protection probable. Associated with longevity.

VERY LOW-DENSITY LIPOPROTEINS (VLDL) AND LOW-DENSITY LIPOPROTEINS (LDL)

Desirable Values—LDL

Adults
    <130 mg/dL, or <3.4 mmol/L: desirable LDL-cholesterol
    140–159 mg/dL, or 3.4–4.1 mmol/L: borderline high-risk LDL-cholesterol
    >160 mg/dL, or >4.1 mmol/L: high-risk LDL-cholesterol
Children and adolescents
    <110 mg/dL, or <2.8 mmol/L: Desirable LDL-cholesterol
    110–129 mg/dL, or 2.8–3.4 mmol/L: Borderline high-risk LDL-cholesterol
    >130 mg/dL, or >3.4 mmol/L: High-risk LDL-cholesterol

TRIGLYCERIDES

Normal Values

Age (y)	Male (mg/dL)	Female (mg/dL)
0–9	30–100	35–110
9–14	32–125	37–131
14–20	37–148	39–124
>20	40–160	35–135

••

Values are age and diet related.

CHAPTER 5

Neurologic
Reference Facts

TABLE 5-1 Cranial Nerve Function and Assessment

Number	Name	Function	Method of Assessment
I	Olfactory	Sense of smell	Ask patient to identify different mild aromas, such as vanilla, coffee, chocolate, cloves.
II	Optic	Vision	Ask patient to read Snellen chart.
III	Oculomotor	Pupillary reflex	Assess pupil reaction to penlight.
		Extraocular eye movement	Assess directions of gaze by holding your finger 18 inches from patient's face. Ask patient to follow your finger up and down and side to side.
IV	Trochlear	Lateral and downward movement of eyeball	Assess directions of gaze. Test with cranial nerve II.
V	Trigeminal	Sensation to cornea, skin of face, nasal mucosa	Lightly touch cotton swab to lateral sclera of eye to elicit blink. Measure sensation of touch and pain on face using cotton wisp and pin.

(continued)

TABLE 5-1 Cranial Nerve Function and Assessment (Continued)

Number	Name	Function	Method of Assessment
VI	Abducens	Lateral movement of eyeball	Assess directions of gaze. Test with cranial nerve III.
VII	Facial	Facial expression	Ask patient to smile, frown, raise eyebrows.
		Taste—anterior two thirds of tongue	Ask patient to identify different tastes on tip and sides of tongue: sugar (sweet), salt, lemon juice (sour).
VIII	Auditory	Hearing	Assess ability to hear spoken word.
IX	Glossopharyngeal	Taste—posterior tongue	Ask patient to identify different tastes on back of tongue as above.
		Swallowing	Place a tongue blade on posterior tongue while patient says "ah" to elicit a gag response.
		Movement of tongue	Ask patient to move tongue up and down, and side to side.
X	Vagus	Swallowing	Assess with cranial nerve IX by observing palate and pharynx move as patient says "ah."
		Movement of vocal cords	
		Sensation of pharynx	
XI	Spinal accessory	Head and shoulder movement	Ask patient to turn head side to side and shrug shoulders against resistance from examiner's hands.
XII	Hypoglossal	Tongue position	Ask patient to stick out tongue to midline, then move it side to side.

TABLE 5-2 Mini-Mental Status Exam
....

Maximum Score	Factor
	Orientation
5	What is the (year) (season) (date) (day) (month)?
5	Where are we (state) (county) (town) (hospital) (floor)?
	Registration
3	Name three objects; allow 1 second to say each. Then, ask the patient to repeat the three objects after you have said them. Give one point for each correct answer. Repeat until the patient learns all three. Count trials and record number.
	Attention and calculation
5	Ask the patient to begin with 100 and count backward by sevens (stop after five answers). Alternatively, spell "world" backward.
	Recall
3	Ask the patient to repeat the three objects that you previously asked him or her to remember.
	Language
2	Show the patient a pencil and a watch and ask him or her to name them.
1	Ask the patient to repeat the following: "No ifs, ands, or buts."
3	Give the patient a three-stage command: "Take a paper in your right hand, fold it in half, and put it on the floor."
1	Show the patient the written item "Close your eyes" and ask the patient to read and obey it.
1	Tell the patient to write a sentence.
1	Tell the patient to copy a design (complex polygon).
30	Total score possible

Scoring: 24 to 30 correct—intact cognitive function
        20 to 23 correct—mild cognitive impairment
        16 to 19 correct—moderate cognitive impairment
        15 or less correct—severe cognitive impairment
....

Folstein MF, Folstein SE, McHugh PR. "Mini-mental state." A practical method for grading the cognitive state of patients for the clinician. *J Psychiatr Res* 1975; 12 (3), 189–98.

TABLE 5-3 The Glasgow Coma Scale

Response	Score
BEST EYE-OPENING RESPONSE	
Spontaneously	4
To speech	3
To pain	2
No response	1
BEST VERBAL RESPONSE	
Oriented	5
Confused conversation	4
Inappropriate words	3
Garbled sounds	2
No response	1
BEST MOTOR RESPONSE	
Obeys commands	6
Localizes stimuli	5
Withdrawal from stimulus	4
Abnormal flexion (decorticate)	3
Abnormal extension (decerebrate)	2
No response	1

In each of the three categories, the patient's best response is assigned a score. When totaled, the score provides an overall view of the patient's level of consciousness.

BICEPS REFLEX

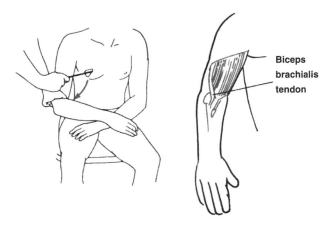

With reflex hammer, tap your thumb placed over biceps tendon with client's arm flexed (tests nerve roots C5, C6). Biceps contracts (1+, 2+, 3+ biceps reflex)

BRACHIORADIALIS REFLEX

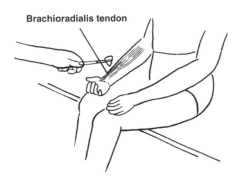

Tap brachioradialis tendon just above the wrist on radial side with client's arm resting midway between supination and pronation (tests nerve roots C5, C6). Elbow flexes with pronation of forearm (1+, 2+, 3+ brachioradialis reflex)

FIGURE 5-1 Assessing deep tendon reflexes. *(continued)*

TRICEPS REFLEX

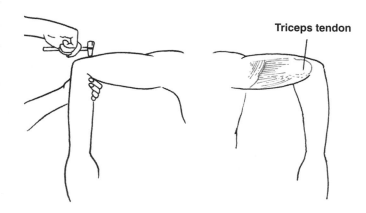

Tap triceps tendon (just above elbow) with client's arm abducted and forearm hanging freely (tests nerve roots C6, C7, C8). Elbow extends (1+, 2+, 3+ triceps reflex)

PATELLAR REFLEX

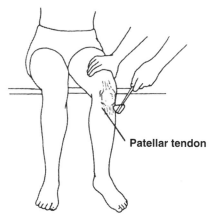

Tap patellar tendon with client's knee flexed and thigh stabilized (tests nerve roots L2 and L3). Extension of knee (1+, 2+, 3+ patella reflex)

FIGURE 5-1 (Continued)

ACHILLES REFLEX

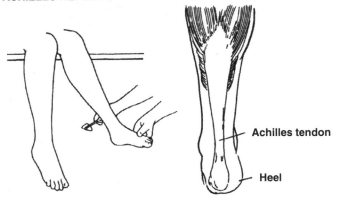

Tap Achilles tendon with client's foot slightly dorsiflexed and stabilized (tests nerve roots S1, S2). Plantar flexion of foot (1+, 2+,
3+ Achilles reflex)

FIGURE 5-1 (Continued)

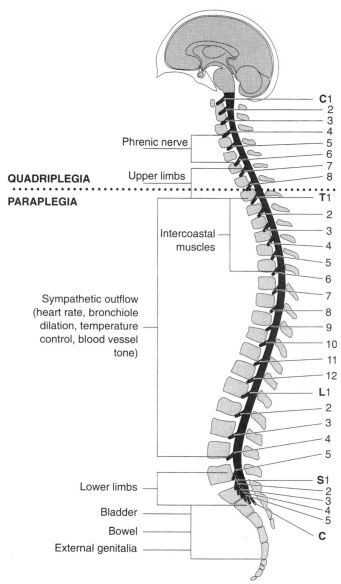

FIGURE 5-2 Levels of spinal cord innervation.

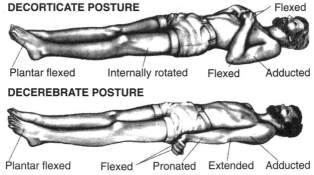

FIGURE 5-3 Posturing positions.

TABLE 5-4 Normal CSF Values

Volume   90–150 mL; child: 60–100 mL
Appearance   Crystal clear, colorless
Pressure   50–180 mm H_2O
Total cell count RBCs: 0

		Adults	**Newborn (0–14 d)**
	WBCs	0–5 cells	0–30 cells
	Diff		
	Lymphs	40%–80%	5%–35%
	Monos	15%–45%	50%–90%
	Polys	0%–6%	0%–8%

Specific gravity   1.006–1.008
Osmolality   280–290 mOsm/kg

CLINICAL TESTS

Glucose	40–70 mg/dL	
Protein		
Lumbar	Neonates	15–100 mg/dL
	3 mo–60 y	15–45 mg/dL
	>60 y	15–60 mg/dL
Cisternal		15–25 mg/dL
Ventricular		15–16 mg/dL
Lactic acid	10–24 mg/dL	
Glutamine	0.4–1.1 μmol/mL	
Albumin	10–30 mg/dL	

(continued)

TABLE 5-4 Normal CSF Values (Continued)

CLINICAL TESTS

Urea nitrogen	5–25 mg/dL
Creatinine	0.5–1.2 mg/dL
Cholesterol	0.2–0.6 mg/dL
Uric acid	0.5–4.5 mg/dL
Bilirubin	0 (none)
LDH	1/10 that of serum LDH

ELECTROLYTES AND pH

pH	7.30–7.40
Chloride	118–132 mEq/L
Sodium	144–154 mEq/L
Potassium	2.0–3.5 mEq/L
CO_2 content	25–30 mEq/L (mmol)
Pco_2	42–53 mm Hg
Po_2	40–44 mm Hg
Calcium	2.1–2.7 mEq/L
Magnesium	2.4 mEq/L

SEROLOGY AND MICROBIOLOGY

VDRL	Negative
Bacteria	None present
Viruses	None present

CHAPTER 6

Gastrointestinal Reference Facts

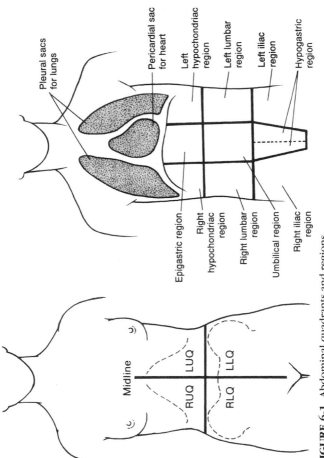

Pleural sacs for lungs

Pericardial sac for heart

Left hypochondriac region

Left lumbar region

Left iliac region

Hypogastric region

Epigastric region

Right hypochondriac region

Right lumbar region

Umbilical region

Right iliac region

Midline

RUQ | LUQ

RLQ | LLQ

FIGURE 6-1 Abdominal quadrants and regions.

91

TABLE 6-1 Special Diets

It may be necessary to modify the diet's texture, consistency, calories, or other nutrients if the client has had surgery or has a medical condition that requires an altered diet. Modifications of consistency are clear liquid, full liquid, soft, and mechanical soft.

Clear liquid This diet includes only liquids that lack residue, such as juices without pulp (eg, apple, cranberry), tea, gelatin, soda pop, and clear broth.

Full liquid A full liquid diet includes all fluids and foods that become liquid at room temperature (eg, ice cream, sherbet).

Soft Soft diets include soft foods and those with reduced fiber content, which require less energy for digestion. Soft diets are appropriate for the person who has difficulty chewing or who has no teeth. *Mechanical soft* diets are further chopped or pureed. Soft diets also may be used for the postoperative client as the diet progresses from full liquid.

Diet as tolerated Diet as tolerated is ordered when the client's ability to tolerate certain foods may change, such as during the postoperative period or after GI distress.

DIETARY MODIFICATIONS FOR DISEASES

Disease	Modification
Renal disease	Restrict intake of sodium, potassium, protein, and possibly fluids.
Liver disease (cirrhosis)	Restrict intake of sodium; increase intake of protein, unless hepatic coma is pending; then protein is virtually eliminated.
Congestive heart failure	Restrict intake of sodium and calories.
Coronary artery disease	Restrict intake of sodium, calories, and fats (saturated fats and cholesterol).
Burns	Increase intake of calories, protein, vitamin C, and the B-complex vitamins.
Respiratory (emphysema)	A soft, high-calorie, high-protein diet is recommended.
Tuberculosis	Increase intake of protein, calories, calcium, and vitamin A.
Hypertension	Restrict sodium intake; lose weight, if appropriate.

TABLE 6-2 Commonly Used Enema Solutions

Solution	Amount	Action	Time to Take Effect	Adverse Effects
Tap water (hypotonic)	500–1000 mL	Distends intestine, increases peristalsis, softens stool	15 min	Fluid and electrolyte imbalance, water intoxication
Normal saline (isotonic)	500–1000 mL	Distends intestine, increases peristalsis, softens stool	15 min	Fluid and electrolyte imbalance, sodium retention
Soap	500–1000 mL (concentrate at 3–5 mL/1000 mL)	Distends intestine, irritates intestinal mucosa, softens stool	10–15 min	Rectal mucosa irritation or damage
Hypertonic	70–130 mL	Distends intestine, irritates intestinal mucosa	5–10 min	Sodium retention
Oil (mineral, olive, or cottonseed oil)	150–200 mL	Lubricates stool and intestinal mucosa	30 min	

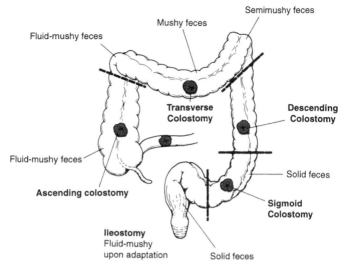

FIGURE 6-2 Types of ostomies and stool characteristics.

TABLE 6-3 Common Types of Gastrointestinal Tubes*

Tube Type	Description	Purpose	Nursing Considerations
Levin or Wangensteen	Single lumen Short tube (20–24 in) Multiple holes at distal tip	Provides intermittent suction of gastric contents	Irrigate frequently with small amounts of saline or air to keep patent.
Salem Sump	Double lumen (two ports) Short tube (20–24 in) Multiple holes at distal tip	One port provides air flow. Second port allows suction of gastric contents with continuous suction	Clear the air port with air to keep open and prevent distal tip from sucking against the wall of the stomach and causing irritation.
Sengstaken-Blakemore	Triple lumens consisting of one channel and two balloons	One channel provides irrigation and in-termittent suction of gastric contents. One balloon provides pressure on the car-diac sphincter area when inflated just inside the stomach. Second balloon provides pressure along the wall of the esophagus to stop bleeding varices.	Nasotracheal suction is often needed, because swallowing is impossible.

* Mercury-weighted tubes are no longer used for any internal body placement (because of the risk of mercury poisoning). Tungsten-weighted tubes may be used.

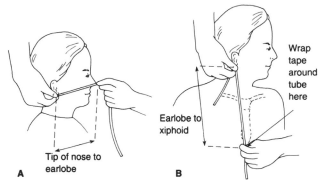

FIGURE 6-3 Estimating NG tube length. Measure distance from tip of nose to earlobe, placing the rounded end of the tubing at earlobe (*A*). Continue measurement from earlobe to sternal notch (*B*). Mark location of sternal notch along the tubing with small strip of tape.

TABLE 6-4 Complications of Enteral Feedings

Complications	Causes	Interventions
Tube displacement	Tube migration into esophagus	Observe for eructation of air when injecting air to test for tube placement in stomach.
		Aspirate for gastric contents; if none is obtained, suspect esophageal placement.
		Advance tube and auscultate for "whooshing" sound of air entering stomach as well as aspiration of gastric contents.
	Tube placement into respiratory tract	Observe for gagging, dyspnea, inability to speak, coughing when tube insertion attempted.
		Aspirate for gastric contents; if pH >6, suspect respiratory tract placement.
		Obtain chest x-ray.*

TABLE 6-4 Complications of Enteral Feedings (Continued)

••

Complications	Causes	Interventions
Tube displacement *(cont.)*		Withdraw tube and attempt reinsertion with patient's head flexed forward.*
Tube obstruction	Tube kinking	Obtain chest x-ray to confirm and withdraw and reinsert new tube.*
	Tube clogging	Flush tube every 4 hours with 30 mL of water and after administration of intermittent feeding and medication.
		Administer medications in liquid form if possible. Crush medications finely.
Vomiting	Tube migration into esophagus	See interventions for tube migration.
	Decreased absorption	Auscultate for decreased bowel sounds. Observe for abdominal distention.
		Consider decreasing amount of tube feeding. Change type of feeding to one requiring less digestive effort and a lower fat content.*
		Consider administration on a continuous basis.*
		Consider placement of a small-bore, weighted-tip nasointestinal tube.*
	Rapid rate of infusion	Administer no faster than 200–300 mL over 10–20 minutes.
		Consider administration on a continuous basis.*
	Excessive infusion of air	If giving a bolus feeding, pinch tubing off when refilling syringe with formula.

(continued)

TABLE 6-4 Complications of Enteral Feedings (Continued)

Complications	Causes	Interventions
Vomiting *(cont.)*		If giving continuous feeding, make certain bag does not empty before closing off tubing.
	Patient position	Maintain patient at 30–45-degree angle of head elevation during and 30–60 minutes after feeding. If administering continuous feeding, maintain head elevation at all times.
Diarrhea	Drug therapy	Evaluate drug regimen for possible causes of drug-induced diarrhea from antibiotics, elixirs with high osmolarity, H_2-blockers, magnesium-containing antacids.
	Hypoalbuminemia	Check serum albumin levels. Administer formula requiring less digestion.*
	High osmolarity of formula	Begin administration of formula at slow rate.*
		Consider continuous rather than intermittent feeding.*
		Consider diluting formula with water and gradually increasing concentration.*
	Lactose intolerance	Administer lactose-free formula.*
	Bacterial contamination of formula	Change administration set daily or per agency protocol.
		Maintain strict medical asepsis, including careful hand washing before administration of formula.
		Allow formula to hang no longer than 8 hours.

TABLE 6-4 Complications of Enteral Feedings (Continued)

●●●

Complications	Causes	Interventions
Diarrhea *(cont.)*	Rapid infusion rate	Administer slowly; consider continuous rather than intermittent infusion.*
Constipation	Lack of fiber	Administer formula with fiber.*
	Decreased fluid intake	Increase intake of water.*
	Drug therapy	Evaluate drug regimen for possible cause, including aluminum-containing antacids.
Hyperglycemia	High caloric density formula (1.5–2 kcal/mL)	Monitor serum glucose, assess for dehydration due to hyperosmotic diuresis; observe for symptoms of hyperglycemia, including polyuria, polydipsia. Change formula to lower calorie content.* Administer insulin.* Observe for hypercapnea (increased respirations, elevated P_{CO_2}).
Electrolyte imbalance Hypernatremia	Dehydration	Assess for signs and symptoms of dehydration (I&O, daily weights, skin turgor, blood urea nitrogen, central venous pressure, tachycardia, hypotension). Rehydrate with D5W and/or hypotonic saline solutions.*
Hyponatremia	Overhydration	Observe for signs and symptoms of hypervolemia (shortness of breath, rales, I&O, daily weight, peripheral edema, elevated CVP). Observe for signs and symptoms of hyponatremia *(continued)*

TABLE 6-4 Complications of Enteral Feedings (Continued)

Complications	Causes	Interventions
Electrolyte imbalance *(cont.)* Hyponatremia *(cont.)*		(lethargy, headaches, mental status change, nausea, vomiting, abdominal cramping). Replace sodium, administer diuretics, restrict fluids.*
Hyperkalemia	Metabolic acidosis/renal insufficiency	Observe for signs and symptoms of hyperkalemia (dysrhythmias, diarrhea, muscle weakness). Treat underlying cause. Administer exchange resin, glucose, and insulin.*
Hypokalemia	Diarrhea	See interventions for diarrhea. If severe, replace potassium.*

H₂: histamine; I&O: intake and output; CVP: central venous pressure.
* Obtain orders from health care provider.

TABLE 6-5 Complications of Administration of Total Nutrient Admixture (TNA) and Treatment

Complications	Causes	Interventions
Sepsis	High glucose content of fluid Venous access device contamination	Monitor temperature, WBC count, insertion site for signs and symptoms of infection. Maintain strict surgical asepsis when changing dressing and tubing. Consider decreasing glucose content of fluid.* Consider removal of venous access device with replacement in alternate site.* If blood cultures positive, consider institution of antibiotic therapy.*

TABLE 6-5 Complications of Administration of Total Nutrient Admixture (TNA) and Treatment (Continued)

Complications	Causes	Interventions
Electrolyte imbalance	Iatrogenic Effect of underlying diseases, eg, fistula, diarrhea, vomiting	Monitor electrolyte levels at least every 2–3 days. Monitor signs and symptoms of electrolyte imbalance. Treat underlying cause.* Change concentration of electrolytes in TNA as necessary to address blood levels.*
Hyperglycemia	High glucose content of fluid Insufficient insulin secretion	Monitor blood glucose frequently. Decrease glucose content of fluid if possible.* Administer exogenous insulin per addition to TNA, subcutaneously or through a separate intravenous drip.*
Hypoglycemia	Abrupt discontinuation of TNA administered through a central vessel	After discontinuation of centrally administered TNA, start $D_{10}W$ at the same rate.*
Hypervolemia	Iatrogenic Underlying disease, eg, CHF, renal failure	Monitor intake and output, daily weights, CVP, breath sounds, peripheral edema. Consider administering more concentrated TNA solution.*
Hyperosmolar diuresis	High osmolarity of TNA	Monitor intake and output, daily weights, CVP. Consider decreasing concentration or amount of fluid administered.*
Hepatic dysfunction	High concentration of carbohydrates and/or fats relative to protein in TNA	Monitor liver function tests, triglyceride levels, presence of jaundice. Consider alteration in formula content.*
Hypercapnea	High carbohydrate content of fluid	Consider changing formula to increase the proportion of fat relative to carbohydrate.

(continued)

TABLE 6-5 **Complications of Administration of Total Nutrient Admixture (TNA) and Treatment** (Continued)

Complications	Causes	Interventions
Lipid intolerance	Low-birth-weight or premature infant	Monitor for bleeding (check stools for occult blood, co-agulation studies, platelet levels). Monitor O_2 levels for impaired oxygenation.
	History of liver disease History of elevated triglycerides	Monitor for fat overload syndrome: monitor triglyceride levels and liver function tests, hepatosplenomegaly, decreased coagulation, cyanosis, dyspnea. Monitor allergic reaction: nausea, vomiting, headache, chest pain, back pain, fever. Administer lipid-containing solutions slowly initially, while observing for symptoms.
Lipid particulate aggregation	Unstable mixture of dextrose solution with lipid emulsion	Observe for cracking or creaming of fluid, and avoid use of fluid with these characteristics.

WBC: white blood cell; CHF: congestive heart failure; CVP: central venous pressure.
* Obtain orders from health care provider.

TABLE 6-6 Liver Function Studies

Test and Purpose	Normal	Clinical and Nursing Significance
BILE FORMATION AND SECRETION		
1. *Serum bilirubin (van den Bergh's reaction)* Measures bilirubin in the blood; this determines the ability of the liver to take up, conjugate, and excrete bilirubin. Bilirubin is a product of the breakdown of hemoglobin.		
Direct (conjugated)—soluble in water	0–5.1 μmol/L	Abnormal in biliary and liver disease, causing jaundice clinically
Indirect (unconjugated)—insoluble in water	0–14 μmol/L	Abnormal in hemolysis and in functional disorders of uptake or conjugation.
Total serum bilirubin	1.7–20.5 μmol/L.	
2. *Urine bilirubin* Not normally found in urine, but if direct serum bilirubin is elevated, some spills into urine.	None (0)	Mahogany-colored urine; when specimen is shaken, yellow-tinted foam can be observed. Confirm with Ictotest tablet or Dipstick. If phenazopyridine (Pyridium) is being taken, there may be a false-positive bilirubin result. (Mark laboratory slip if this medication is being taken)

(continued)

103

TABLE 6-6 Liver Function Studies (Continued)

Test and Purpose	Normal	Clinical and Nursing Significance
BILE FORMATION AND SECRETION (cont.)		
3. *Urobilinogen* Formed in small intestine by action of bacteria on bilirubin. Related to amount of bilirubin excreted into bile.	Urine urobilinogen up to 0.09–4.23 µmol/24 h Fecal urobilinogen 0.068–0.34 mmol/24 h	Urine specimen is collected over 2-h period after lunch. Place specimen in dark brown container and send it to laboratory immediately to prevent decomposition. If the patient is receiving antimicrobials, mark laboratory slip to this effect, as production of urobilinogen can be falsely reduced.
PROTEIN STUDIES		
1. *Albumin and globulin measurement* Is of greater significance than total protein measurement		As one increases, the other decreases; hence,
Albumin—produced by liver cells	35–55 g/L	Albumin ↓ cirrhosis chronic hepatitis
Globulin—produced in lymph nodes, spleen, and bone marrow and Kupffer's cells of liver	15–30 g/L	Globulin ↑ cirrhosis chronic obstructive jaundice viral hepatitis
Total serum protein	60–80 g/L	
2. *Prothrombin time (PT)* Prothrombin and other clotting factors are manufactured in the liver; its rate is	100% of control	Prothrombin time may be prolonged in liver disease, in which case it will not return to normal with vitamin K. It may also

104

be prolonged in malabsorption of fat and fat-soluble vitamins, in which case it will return to normal with vitamin K.

FAT METABOLISM

1. *Cholesterol*
   It is possible to measure lipid metabolism by determining serum cholesterol levels.

3.90–6.50 mmol/L.
Esters = 60% of total

Serum cholesterol level is decreased in parenchymal liver disease. Serum lipid level is increased in biliary obstruction.

LIVER DETOXIFICATION

1. *Serum alkaline phosphatase*
   Because bile disposes this enzyme, any impairment of liver cell excretory function will cause an elevation. In cholestasis or obstruction, increased synthesis of enzyme causes very high levels in blood.

20–90 U/L at 30°C

Abnormalities: The level is elevated to more than 3 times normal in obstructive jaundice, intrahepatic cholestasis, liver metastasis, or granulomas. Also elevated in osteoblastic diseases, Paget's disease, and hyperparathyroidism.

ENZYME PRODUCTION

Aspartate aminotransferase or AST (formerly SGOT)

4.8–19 U/L.

Alanine aminotransferase or ALT (formerly SGPT)

2.4–7 U/L

Lactic dehydrogenase (LDH)

80–192 U/L.

Gamma glutamyl transpeptidase (GGT)

0–30 U/L at 30° C

An elevation in these enzymes indicates liver cell damage.
Note: Opiates may also cause a rise in AST and ALT.
Aspirin may cause an increase or decrease in AST and ALT.

Enzyme found in liver, kidney, heart, pancreas, spleen, brain. An elevation confirms hepatic involvement in the presence of an elevated alkaline phosphatase.

(continued)

TABLE 6-6 Liver Function Studies (Continued)

Test and Purpose	Normal	Clinical and Nursing Significance
ENZYME PRODUCTION (cont.)		
Ammonia (serum)	11.1–67.0 µmol/L	Ammonia levels rise when the liver is unable to convert it to urea.
Bile acids radioimmunoassay (after cholecystokinin stimulation)		Elevated serum bile acids are seen in the presence of hepatic diseases.
Total	35.0–148.0 mmol/L.	
Chenodeoxycholic acid	10.0–61.4 mmol/L	
Cholic acid	6.8–81.0 mmol/L	
Deoxycholic acid	2.0–18.0 mmol/L	
Lithocholic acid	0.8–2.0 mmol/L	

SGOT: serum glutamic oxaloacetic transaminase; SGPT: serum glutamic pyruvic transaminase.

CHAPTER 7

Fluid and Electrolyte Reference Facts

TABLE 7-1 Assessment Parameters for Fluid, Electrolyte, and Acid–Base Balance

Assessment Parameters	Nursing Considerations	Findings in Healthy Adult	Significant Findings
Comparison of total intake and output of fluids	• Records may be initiated by the nurse for any client with a real or potential water or electrolyte problem. • Intake should include all fluids taken into the body (oral fluids, foods that are liquid at room temperature, IV fluids, subcutaneous fluids, fluids instilled into drainage tubes as irrigants, tube feeding solutions and water, even enema solutions in clients requiring strict fluid intake recording). • Output should include urine, vomitus, diarrhea, drainage from fistulas, and drainage from suction apparatus. Perspiration and drainage from lesions should be noted and	• Fluid intake about equals fluid output—when averaged over 2 or 3 days. • Range of 1500 to 3500 mL fluid intake and loss; 2000 mL is average adult intake and loss per day. • Output of urine normally approximates the ingestion of liquids; water from food and oxidation is balanced by the water loss through feces, the skin, and the respiratory process.	• When the total intake is substantially less than the total output, the client is in danger of fluid volume deficit. • When the total intake is substantially more than the total output, the client is in danger of fluid volume excess.

(continued)

TABLE 7-1 Assessment Parameters for Fluid, Electrolyte, and Acid–Base Balance (Continued)

Assessment Parameters	Nursing Considerations	Findings in Healthy Adult	Significant Findings
Comparison of total intake and output of fluids (cont.)	estimated. Prolonged hyperventilation should also be noted because it is an important route of water vapor loss.		
Urine volume and concentration	• Measure all fluid losses according to routes. • Use a device calibrated for small volumes of urine when hourly urine volumes need to be measured. • Account for factors that can alter urinary output: 1. Amount of fluid intake 2. Losses from skin, lungs, and GI tract 3. Amount of waste products for excretions 4. Renal concentrating ability 5. Blood volume	• Normal urinary output is about 1 mL/kg of body weight per hour (for the average adult: 1500 mL/24 h, which is equivalent to about 40 to 80 mL/h). • Stress may diminish the 24-hour urine volume in the adult to 750 to 1000 mL (or 30 to 50 mL/h) because of increased aldosterone and ADH secretion. • The range of specific gravity is from 1.003 to 1.035. Urine osmolality ranges between 500 mOsm and 800 mOsm/kg (mmol/kg).	• A low urine volume with a high specific gravity indicates fluid volume deficit. • A low urine volume with a low specific gravity indicates renal disease. • A high urine volume suggests fluid volume excess. • Urine volume is increased in conditions with high solute loads, such as diabetes mellitus, high protein tube feedings, and fever. • Hypovolemia causes decreased renal perfusion and thus oliguria; hypervolemia causes increased urinary

Body weight

- Hormonal influences (primarily aldosterone and ADH)

- Because of the common inaccuracies in recording intake and output, body weight is believed to be a more accurate indicator of fluid gained and lost.

- Guidelines for weighing clients:
  1. Use the same scale each time.
  2. Measure weight at the same time each day: in the morning before breakfast and after voiding.
  3. Be sure the client is wearing the same, or similar clothing (clothing should be dry).
  4. If the client is unable to stand on a small, portable scale, use a bed scale.

- A client may have a severe fluid volume deficit even though body weight is essentially unchanged

- A client's dry weight should remain relatively stable.

- Rapid variations in weight closely reflect changes in body fluid volume.

- A rapid loss of body weight occurs when the total fluid intake is less than the total fluid output.
  1. Rapid loss of 2% total body weight (TBW) indicates mild fluid volume deficit.
  2. Rapid loss of 5% TBW indicates moderate fluid volume deficit.
  3. Rapid loss of 8% or more of TBW indicates severe fluid volume deficit.

- A rapid gain of body weight occurs when the total fluid intake is greater than the total fluid output.
  1. Rapid gain of 2% TBW indicates mild fluid volume excess.
  2. Rapid gain of 5% TBW indicates

volume if the kidneys are functioning normally.

(continued)

111

TABLE 7-1 Assessment Parameters for Fluid, Electrolyte, and Acid–Base Balance (Continued)

Assessment Parameters	Nursing Considerations	Findings in Healthy Adult	Significant Findings
Body weight (cont.)	when there is a third-space loss of body fluid.		moderate fluid volume excess. 3. Rapid gain of 8% or more of TBW indicates severe fluid volume excess. • A rapid gain or loss of 1 kg (2.2 lb) of body weight is about equal to the gain or loss of 1 L of fluid.
Skin turgor (elasticity)	• Pinch the client's skin over the sternum, inner aspect of the thighs, or forehead. • Some prefer to test skin turgor in children over the abdominal area and on the medial aspect of the thighs. • Skin turgor can vary with age, nutritional state, and even race and complexion. Observations are most meaningful if done sequentially	• Pinched skin immediately falls back to its normal position when released. • Reduced skin turgor is common in older clients (those more than 55 to 60 years of age) because of a primary decrease in skin elasticity.	• In a person with a fluid volume deficit, the skin flattens more slowly after the pinch is released; the skin may remain elevated for many seconds. • Severe malnutrition, particularly in infants, can cause depressed skin turgor even in the absence of fluid depletion.

Tongue turgor	before the development of a fluid balance abnormality. • Unlike skin turgor, tongue turgor is not affected appreciably by age and thus is a useful assessment for all age groups.	• Tongue has one longitudinal furrow.	• In the person with fluid volume deficit there are additional longitudinal furrows and the tongue is smaller. • Sodium excess causes the tongue to look red and swollen.
Moisture and oral cavity	• A dry mouth may be the result of fluid volume deficit or of mouth breathing. When in doubt, the nurse should run a finger along the oral cavity and feel the membrane where the cheek and gum meet; dryness in this area indicates a true fluid volume deficit.	• Mucous membranes in oral cavity are moist.	• Dryness of the membrane where the cheek and gum meet indicates fluid volume deficit. • Dry sticky mucous membranes are noted in sodium excess. (The oral cavity feels like flypaper.)
Tearing and salivation		• Tearing and salivation decrease normally with age.	• The absence of tearing and salivation in a child is a sign of fluid volume deficit; it becomes obvious with a fluid loss of 5% of TBW.
Appearance of skin and skin temperature			• Metabolic acidosis can cause warm, flushed skin (due to peripheral vasodilation).

(continued)

113

TABLE 7-1 Assessment Parameters for Fluid, Electrolyte, and Acid–Base Balance (Continued)

Assessment Parameters	Nursing Considerations	Findings in Healthy Adult	Significant Findings
Appearance of skin and skin temperature (*cont.*)			• Severe fluid volume deficit causes the skin to be pale and cool as a result of vasoconstriction, which occurs to compensate for hypovolemia.
Facial appearance			• A person with a severe fluid volume deficit has a pinched and drawn facial expression. • A fluid volume deficit of 10% of body weight causes decreased intraocular pressure, causing the eyes to appear sunken and to feel soft to the touch.
Edema (excessive accumulation of interstitial fluid)	• Pitting edema (phenomenon manifested by a small depression that remains after one's finger is pressed over an edematous area and then	• No edema	• Clinically edema is not usually apparent in the adult until the retention of 5 to 10 lb of excess fluid occurs.

- removed) may be indicated by using plus signs to indicate the amount, ranging from +1 (barely perceptible edema) to +4 (severe edema).
- Measurement of an extremity or body part with a millimeter tape, in the same area each day, is a more exact method of measurement.
- An excess of interstitial fluid may accumulate predominantly in the lower extremities of ambulatory clients and in the presacral region of bedridden clients.
- The presence of periorbital (around the eyes) edema or pedal edema should prompt one to look for edema in other parts of the body.

- Pitting edema is not evident until at least a 10% increase in weight has occurred.
- Formation of edema may be localized (as in thrombophlebitis) or generalized (as in heart failure, cirrhosis of liver, or nephrotic syndrome). Edema of congestive heart failure, liver cirrhosis, or nephrotic syndrome is the result of sodium retention.
- There is no peripheral edema with only water retention (as occurs with excessive secretions of ADH). Instead, there is a cellular swelling that can be detected by pressing one's finger over the sternum and producing a visible fingerprint.

Body temperature

- Because fever increases the loss of body fluids it is important that temperature elevations be detected early and appropriate interventions be taken.
- Body temperature and other vital

Baseline temperature: diurnal variations

- There is an elevation of body temperature in hypernatremia (dehydration) probably related to lack of available fluid for sweating. Also, dehydration has a direct effect on the hypothalamus.

(continued)

TABLE 7-1 Assessment Parameters for Fluid, Electrolyte, and Acid–Base Balance (Continued)

Assessment Parameters	Nursing Considerations	Findings in Healthy Adult	Significant Findings

Edema (excessive accumulation of interstitial fluid) *(cont.)*	signs should be assessed at the nurse's discretion.		• There is a decrease in body temperature in fluid volume deficit, when uncomplicated by infection (probably as a result of decreased metabolism).
			
			• Fever increases the loss of body fluids.
			
			  1. Increased metabolism produces more metabolic wastes and increased urinary output.
			
			  2. Fever also causes hyperpnea, an increase in breathing that results in extra vapor loss through the lungs.
			
			• A temperature elevation between 101°F (38.3°C) and 103°F (39.4°C) increases the 24-hour fluid requirement by at least 500 mL, and a tem-

		perature above 103°F increases it by at least 1000 mL.
	• Baseline pulse rate, rhythm, and volume	• Tachycardia is usually the earliest sign of the decreased vascular volume associated with fluid volume deficit. It may also be associated with deficits of magnesium or potassium.
		• Excesses of magnesium or potassium can cause decreased heart rate.
		• Irregular pulse rates also occur with potassium imbalances and magnesium deficit.
		• Pulse volume is decreased in fluid volume deficit and increased in fluid volume excess.
Respirations	• Baseline respiratory rate, rhythm, and qualities	• Deep, rapid respirations may be a compensatory mechanism for metabolic acidosis or a primary disorder causing respiratory alkalosis.
		• Slow, shallow respirations may be a compensatory mechanism for

(continued)

117

TABLE 7-1 Assessment Parameters for Fluid, Electrolyte, and Acid-Base Balance (Continued)

Assessment Parameters	Nursing Considerations	Findings in Healthy Adult	Significant Findings
Respirations (cont.)			• metabolic alkalosis or a primary disorder causing respiratory acidosis. • Weakness or paralysis of respiratory muscles is likely in severe hypokalemia or hyperkalemia and in severe magnesium excess. • Moist crackles, in the absence of cardiopulmonary disease, indicate fluid volume excess.
Blood pressure	• Whenever a fluid imbalance is suspected, check the client's blood pressure while he or she is lying down, sitting, and standing.	• Baseline blood pressure	• A fall in systolic pressure greater than 15 mm Hg from the lying to the sitting or standing position (postural hypotension) usually indicates fluid volume deficit. • Hypotension may occur with magnesium excess (first occurring at a level of 3 to 5 mEq/L).

Neck veins and central venous pressure (CVP)

- The jugular veins provide a built-in manometer for following changes in CVP.
- To estimate CVP, the nurse:
  1. Positions the client in a semi-Fowler's position (head of bed elevated to a 30- to 45-degree angle), keeping the neck straight.
  2. Removes any of the client's clothing that could constrict the neck or upper chest.
  3. Provides adequate lighting to visualize effectively the external jugular veins on each side of the neck.
  4. Measures the levels to which the veins are distended on the neck or above the level of the manubrium.

- Normally, when the client is supine, the external jugular veins fill to the anterior border of the sternocleidomastoid muscle. With the client positioned sitting at a 45-degree angle, the venous distentions normally should not extend higher than 2 cm above the sternal angle.
- Pressure in the right atrium is usually 0 to 4 cm H_2O; pressure in the vena cava is about 4 to 11 cm H_2O.

- Hypertension can occur with magnesium deficit and with fluid volume excess.
- A low CVP may indicate:
  1. Decreased blood volume
  2. Drug-induced vasodilation (causing pooling of blood in peripheral veins).
- A high CVP may indicate:
  1. Increased blood volume
  2. Heart failure
  3. Vasoconstriction

(continued)

119

TABLE 7-1 Assessment Parameters for Fluid, Electrolyte, and Acid-Base Balance (Continued)

Assessment Parameters	Nursing Considerations	Findings in Healthy Adult	Significant Findings
Neck veins and central venous pressure (CVP) *(cont.)*	• More accurate assessments of blood volume are obtained by measuring CVP with a manometer or by hemodynamic monitoring with a device that measures pressures in both sides of the heart.		
Neuromuscular irritability	• When imbalances in calcium, magnesium, and sodium are suspected it is important to assess clients for increased or decreased neuromuscular irritability. • To test for *Chvostek's sign,* the facial nerve should be percussed about 2 cm anterior to the earlobe. • To test for *Trousseau's sign,* place a blood pressure cuff on the arm	• Negative response • Negative response	• Clients with hypocalcemia or hypomagnesemia respond positively with a unilateral twitching of the facial muscles, including the eyelid and lips. • A positive response is the development of carpal spasm.

and inflate above systolic pressure for 3 minutes.

- A deep tendon reflex is elicited by briskly tapping a partially stretched tendon with a rubber percussion hammer, preferably over the tendon insertion of the muscle. The broad head of the hammer is used to stroke easily accessible tendons and the pointed end for less accessible tendons.

- The muscle being tested should be slightly stretched and the client should be relaxed.

- Reflexes usually are graded on a 0 to 4+ scale
    - 0 = no response
    - 1+ = somewhat diminished, but present
    - 2+ = normal

- The response in the prospective muscle is a sudden contraction (2+).

- Deep tendon reflexes may be hyperactive in the presence of hypocalcemia, hypomagnesemia, hypernatremia, and alkalosis.

- Deep tendon reflexes may be hypoactive in the presence of hypercalcemia, hypermagnesemia, hyponatremia, hypokalemia, and acidosis.

(continued)

TABLE 7-1 Assessment Parameters for Fluid, Electrolyte, and Acid–Base Balance (Continued)

Assessment Parameters	Nursing Considerations	Findings in Healthy Adult	Significant Findings
Neuromuscular irritability *(cont.)*	3+ = brisker than average and possibly but not necessarily indicative of disease 4+ = hyperactive		
Behavior Sensation Fatigue level	• Because these changes are often vague, they are best evaluated in context with specific imbalances.		

(Data from Metheny NM. Fluid and electrolyte balance, 3rd ed. Philadelphia: JB Lippincott, 1996.)

TABLE 7-2 Normal Daily Urine Output during the Lifespan

Age (y)	Output (mL)
Newborn–2	500–600
2–5	500–800
5–8	600–1200
8–14	1000–1500
14 and over	1500

TABLE 7-3 Normal Electrolyte Values

CALCIUM (Ca^{++})

Age	mg/dL	mmol/L
CALCIUM TOTAL		
0–10 d	7.6–10.4	1.90–2.60
10 d–2 y	9.0–11.0	2.25–2.75
2 y–12 y	8.8–10.8	2.20–2.70
12 y–18 y	8.9–10.2	2.10–2.55
Adult	8.6–10.0	2.15–2.50
CALCIUM IONIZED		
Newborn	4.20–5.48	1.05–1.37
1–18 y	4.80–5.52	1.20–1.38
Adult	4.65–5.28	1.16–1.32

CHLORIDE (Cl$^-$)

Newborn	98–113 mmol/L or mEq/L
Adult	98–106 mmol/L or MEq/L

PHOSPHATE (P)/INORGANIC PHOSPHORUS (PO$_4$)

Newborn	4.5–9.0 mg/dL or 1.45–2.91 mmol/L
Child	4.5–5.5 mg/dL or 1.45–1.78 mmol/L
Adult	2.5–4.5 mg/dL or 0.87–1.45 mmol/L

MAGNESIUM (Mg^{++})

Newborn	1.2–1.8 mEq/L or 0.6–0.9 mmol/L
Child	1.4–1.7 mEq/L or 0.71–0.78 mmol/L
Adult	1.3–2.1 mEq/L or 0.65–1.05 mmol/L

(continued)

TABLE 7-3 Normal Electrolyte Values (Continued)

POTASSIUM (K⁺)

Newborn: 0–7 d	3.7–5.9 mmol/L or mEq/L
Infant: 7 d–1 y	4.1–5.3 mmol/L or mEq/L
Child: 1–18 y	3.4–4.7 mmol/L or mEq/L
Adult	3.5–5.3 mmol/L or mEq/L

SODIUM (Na⁺)

Premature infant	140 mEq/L
Full-term infant	133–142 mEq/L
Child: 1–16 y	135–145 mEq/L
Adult	135–145 mmol/L or 135–145 mEq/L

TABLE 7-4 Signs and Symptoms of Electrolyte Imbalances

Related Factors	Defining Characteristics	Nursing Interventions
HYPONATREMIA		
Loss of sodium, as in: • Loss of GI fluids • Use of diuretics • Adrenal insufficiency • Salt-losing nephritis • Osmotic diuresis Gains of water, as in: • Excessive administration of D_5W • Psychogenic polydipsia • Excessive water administration with hypotonic tube feedings Disease states associated with SIADH (a form of hyponatremia): • Oat-cell carcinoma of lung • Carcinoma of duodenum or pancreas	Anorexia Nausea Vomiting Lethargy Confusion Muscle cramps Fingerprinting over sternum Muscular twitching Seizures Coma Papilledema Hemiparesis Serum Na <135 mEq/L Serum osmolality <285 mOsm Urinary Na level varies with cause of hyponatremia	1. Identify clients at risk for hyponatremia. 2. Monitor fluid losses and gains. Look for loss of sodium-containing fluids, particularly in conjunction with low-sodium intake. 3. Monitor for presence of gastrointestinal symptoms, such as anorexia, nausea, vomiting, and abdominal cramping. 4. Monitor for central nervous system changes, such as lethargy, confusion, muscular twitching, and convulsions. Be aware that more severe neurologic signs are associated with very low sodium levels that have fallen rapidly due to water overloading. 5. Monitor laboratory data for serum sodium levels less than normal. 6. Check specific gravity of urine. 7. With clients able to consume a general diet, encourage foods and fluids with a high sodium content. For example, broth made with one beef cube contains about 900 mg of sodium; 8 oz (250 mL) of canned tomato juice contains about 700 mg of sodium.

(continued)

TABLE 7-4 Signs and Symptoms of Electrolyte Imbalances (Continued)

Related Factors	Defining Characteristics	Nursing Interventions

HYPONATREMIA (*cont.*)

Disease states associated with SIADH (*cont.*)

- Head trauma
- Stroke
- Pulmonary disorders (abscesses, pneumonia, tuberculosis)

Pharmacologic agents that may impair renal water excretion, such as:

- Nicotine
- Morphine
- Barbiturates
- Acetaminophen

8. Be familiar with the sodium content of commonly used parenteral fluids. Monitor clients with cardiovascular disease receiving sodium-containing fluids closely for signs of circulatory overload, such as moist rales in the lungs.

9. Use extreme caution when administering hypertonic saline solutions (3% or 5% NaCl). Be aware that these fluids can be *lethal* if infused carelessly.

10. Avoid giving large water supplements to clients receiving isotonic tube feedings, particularly if routes of abnormal sodium loss are present or water is being retained abnormally.

11. Monitor clients with decreased adrenal function for signs of acute adrenocortical insufficiency (adrenal crisis) when they are exposed to severe stress (such as surgery, trauma, emotional upset, excessive heat, or prolonged medical illness). Look for extreme weakness, acute onset of nausea and vomiting, hypotension, confusion, and even shock.

HYPERNATREMIA

Deprivation of water, most common in those unable to perceive or respond to thirst

Hypertonic tube feedings with inadequate water supplements

Increased insensible water loss (as in hyperventilation)

Water diarrhea

Ingestion of salt in unusual amounts

Excessive parenteral administration of sodium-containing solutions:

- Hypertonic saline (3% or 5% NaCl)
- 7.5% sodium bicarbonate
- Isotonic saline

Profuse sweating

Diabetes insipidus

Heatstroke

Drowning in sea water

Thirst

Elevated body temperature

Tongue dry and swollen, sticky mucous membranes

Severe hypernatremia

- Disorientation
- Hallucinations
- Lethargy when undisturbed
- Irritable and hyperreactive when stimulated
- Focal or grand mal seizures, coma

Serum Na >145 mEq/L

Serum osmolality >295 mOsm

Urinary SG >1.015, provided water loss is from nonrenal route

1. Identify clients at risk of hypernatremia.

2. Monitor fluid losses and gains. Look for abnormal losses of water or low water intake, and for large gains of sodium as might occur with ingestion of proprietary drugs with a high sodium content (such as Alka-Seltzer, an effervescent antacid). Also, consider that prescription drugs may have a high sodium content. Of course, one should look for excessive intake of high sodium foods.

3. Monitor for changes in behavior, such as restlessness, disorientation, and lethargy.

4. Look for excessive thirst and elevated body temperature. If present, evaluate in relation to other signs.

5. Monitor serum sodium levels as indicated.

6. Prevent hypernatremia in debilitated clients unable to perceive or respond to thirst by offering them fluids at regular intervals. If fluid intake remains inadequate, consult with the physician to plan an alternate route for intake, either by tube feedings or by the parenteral route.

7. If tube feedings are used, give sufficient water to keep the serum sodium and the BUN level within normal limits. Be aware that the higher the osmolality of the feeding, the greater the need for water supplements.

(continued)

127

TABLE 7-4 Signs and Symptoms of Electrolyte Imbalances (Continued)

Related Factors	Defining Characteristics	Nursing Interventions
HYPERNATREMIA (cont.)		
Hypertonic saline accidentally introduced into maternal circulation during therapeutic abortion		8. Monitor the client's response to corrective parenteral fluids by reviewing serial sodium levels and by observing for changes in neurologic signs. With gradual decrease in the serum sodium level, the neurologic signs should improve, not worsen. Be aware that the serum sodium should be dropped gradually.
HYPOKALEMIA		
Diarrhea	Fatigue	1. Be aware of clients at risk for hypokalemia and monitor for its occurrence. Hypokalemia can be life-threatening; it is important to detect it early.
Vomiting or gastric suction	Anorexia, nausea, and vomiting	
Potassium-losing diuretics (such as furosemide and thiazides)	Muscle weakness	2. Assess digitalized clients at risk for hypokalemia especially closely for symptoms of digitalis toxicity because hypokalemia potentiates the action of digitalis. Be aware that the physician usually prefers to keep the serum potassium level above 3.5 mEq/L in digitalized clients.
Steroid administration	Decreased bowel motility (intestinal ileus)	
Carbenicillin, sodium penicillin, amphotericin B	Cardiac arrhythmias	
Hyperaldosteronism	Increased sensitivity to digitalis toxicity	3. Take measures to prevent hypokalemia when possible.
Hyperalimentation	Polyuria, nocturia, dilute urine (if hypokalemia is prolonged)	a. Prevention may take the form of encouraging extra potassium intake for at-risk client (when the diet allows).
	Mild hyperglycemia	

Poor intake, as in anorexia nervosa, alcoholism, potassium-free parenteral fluids
Osmotic diuresis (as occurs in uncontrolled diabetes mellitus or mannitol administration)
Renal tubular acidosis
Cushing's syndrome

Postural hypotension
Serum K <3.5 mEq/L
Paresthesias or tender muscles
ECG changes:
  Flattened T waves
  ST segment depression

b. When hypokalemia is due to abuse of laxatives or diuretics, education of the client may help alleviate the problem.
4. Administer oral potassium supplements when prescribed.
5. Be aware that clients may not need potassium supplements if they are using salt substitutes because these substances usually contain sizable amounts of potassium. Educate clients regarding the use of salt substitutes.
6. Be thoroughly familiar with the critical facts related to administering potassium intravenously.
7. Be aware that any client experiencing life-threatening symptoms, such as arrhythmias or paralysis, requires urgent replacement of potassium.

HYPERKALEMIA

Pseudohyperkalemia:
- Tight tourniquet
- Hemolysis of sample
- Leukocytosis
- Thrombocytosis

Vague muscular weakness is usually first sign
Cardiac arrhythmias, bradycardia, and heart block can occur
Paresthesias of face, tongue, feet, and hands

1. Be aware of clients at risk for hyperkalemia and monitor for its occurrence. Hyperkalemia is life threatening; it is imperative to detect it early.
2. Take measures to prevent hyperkalemia when possible by following guidelines for administering potassium safely, both intravenously and orally.

(continued)

129

TABLE 7-4 Signs and Symptoms of Electrolyte Imbalances (Continued)

Related Factors	Defining Characteristics	Nursing Interventions
HYPERKALEMIA (cont.)		
Decreased potassium excretion: • Oliguric renal failure • Potassium-conserving diuretics • Hypoaldosteronism High potassium intake, especially in presence of renal insufficiency: • Improper use of oral potassium supplements • Rapid or excessive administration of IV potassium • Rapid transfusion of aged blood • High-dose potassium penicillin • Foods high in potassium (such as dried apricots)	Flaccid muscle paralysis (spreads from legs to trunk and arms; respiratory muscles may be affected) GI symptoms such as nausea, intermittent intestinal colic, or diarrhea may occur ECG changes: tall, peaked T waves, absent P waves, widened QRS complex Serum K >5.0 mEq/L (mmol/L)	a. Follow rules for safe administration of potassium. b. Avoid administration of potassium-conserving diuretics, potassium supplements, or salt substitutes to clients with renal insufficiency. c. Caution clients to use salt substitutes sparingly if they are taking other supplementary forms of potassium or are taking potassium-conserving diuretics (eg, spironolactone, triamterene, and amiloride). d. Caution hyperkalemic clients to avoid foods high in potassium content. Some of these are coffee, cocoa, tea, dried fruits, dried beans, whole-grain breads, and milk desserts. Meat and eggs also contain substantial amounts of potassium. (Foods with minimal potassium content include butter, margarine, cranberry juice or sauce, ginger ale, gumdrops or jellybeans, lollipops, root beer, sugar or honey.) 3. To avoid false reports of hyperkalemia, take the following precautions: a. Avoid prolonged use of tourniquet while drawing blood sample

Shift of potassium out of cells:

- Acidosis
- Tissue trauma
- Malignant cell lysis

b. Do not allow client to exercise extremity immediately before drawing blood sample

c. Take blood sample to laboratory as soon as possible (serum must be separated from cells within 1 hour after collection)

d. Avoid drawing blood specimen from a site above an infusion of potassium solution (or any solution for that matter).

4. Be familiar with usual treatment regimens for hyperkalemia and factors related to their safe implementation.

HYPOCALCEMIA

Surgical hypoparathyroidism (may follow thyroid surgery or radical neck surgery for cancer)	Numbness, tingling of fingers, circumoral region, and toes
Malabsorption	Cramps in muscles of extremities
Vitamin D deficiency	Hyperactive deep-tendon reflexes (such as patellar and triceps)
Acute pancreatitis	Trousseau's sign
Excessive administration of citrated blood	Chvostek's sign
Primary hypoparathyroidism	Mental changes, such as confusion and alterations in mood and memory
Alkalotic states (decreased ionized calcium)	Convulsions (usually generalized but may be focal)
Hyperphosphatemia	Spasm of laryngeal muscles
Medullary carcinoma of thyroid	

1. Be aware of clients at risk for hypocalcemia and monitor for its occurrence.

2. Be prepared to take seizure precautions when hypocalcemia is severe.

3. Monitor condition of airway closely because laryngeal stridor can occur.

4. Take safety precautions if confusion is present.

5. Be aware of factors related to the safe administration of calcium replacement salts.

6. Educate people in high-risk groups for osteoporosis (especially postmenopausal women not on estrogen therapy) as to the need for dietary calcium intake. If adequate amounts are not consumed in the diet (as is often the case), calcium supplements should be considered.

(continued)

TABLE 7-4 Signs and Symptoms of Electrolyte Imbalances (Continued)

Related Factors	Defining Characteristics	Nursing Interventions
HYPOCALCEMIA (cont.)		
Hypoalbuminemia (as in cirrhosis, nephrotic syndrome, and starvation) Hypomagnesemia Decreased ultraviolet exposure	Cardiac manifestations; ECG shows prolonged QT interval Spasms of muscles in abdomen (can simulate acute abdominal emergency) Total serum calcium level <8.5 mg/dL or ionized level below normal (<50%) Sulkowitch's test shows light precipitation	a. Most sources recommend that calcium intake for these individuals be 1000 to 1500 mg each day. Of course, the best way for healthy people to ensure an adequate calcium intake is to eat a wide variety of foods from the four food groups daily. b. As stated in a, calcium supplements may be necessary for people unable to consume enough calcium in the diet, such as those who do not tolerate milk or dairy products well. Numerous preparations can be obtained over the counter, and consumers need advice in selecting suitable products. It appears that calcium is best absorbed when taken in divided doses, rather than all at once. Also, it is suggested that some of the calcium be taken at bedtime because calcium loss accelerates during sleep. (Antacids containing aluminum may increase bone loss, and their use is discouraged in people having bone health problems; among these products are Rolaids, Tempo, Di-Gel, Gaviscon, Gelusil, and Mylanta.) c. Some postmenopausal women are advised by their physicians to take estrogen. For those who cannot take

estrogen, synthetically produced calcitonin is now available by prescription.

d. Encourage people with a tendency to form renal stones to consult their physicians before greatly increasing their calcium intake. Also, it is important to encourage these people to drink no less than 2 to 3 qt of fluid a day to protect against stone formation.

7. Educate people at risk for osteoporosis about the value of regular physical exercise in decreasing bone loss.

8. To prevent osteoporosis in later years, educate young women about the need for a normal diet to ensure adequate calcium intake. Also, discuss the calcium-losing aspects of alcohol and nicotine use.

HYPERCALCEMIA

Hyperparathyroidism	Muscular weakness
Malignant neoplastic disease:	Tiredness, listlessness, lethargy
• Solid tumors with metastases (breast, prostate, and malignant melanomas)	Constipation
	Anorexia, nausea, and vomiting
	Decreased memory span, decreased attention span, and confusion
• Solid tumors without bony metastases (lung, head and neck, and renal tumors)	Polyuria and polydipsia
	Renal stones

1. Be aware of clients at risk for hypercalcemia and monitor for its presence.

2. Increase client mobilization when feasible; recall that immobilization favors hypercalcemia.

3. Encourage the oral intake of sufficient fluids to keep the client well hydrated. Sodium-containing fluids should be given, unless contraindicated by other conditions, because sodium favors calcium excretion.

(continued)

133

TABLE 7-4 Signs and Symptoms of Electrolyte Imbalances (Continued)

Related Factors	Defining Characteristics	Nursing Interventions
HYPERCALCEMIA (cont.)		
• Hematologic tumors (lymphoma, acute leukemia, and myeloma) Prolonged immobilization Large doses of vitamin D Overuse of calcium-containing antacids or calcium supplements Thiazide diuretics Milk–alkali syndrome	Neurotic behavior progressing to frank psychosis may occur (reversible with correction of hypercalcemia) Cardiac arrest may occur in hypercalcemic crisis ECG shows shortened QT interval Bone changes seen on film in chronic hypercalcemia Itching and ocular changes (band keratopathy) Serum calcium >10.5 mg/dL Sulkowitch's test shows dense precipitation	4. Discourage excessive consumption of milk products and other high-calcium foods. 5. Encourage adequate bulk in the diet to offset the tendency for constipation. 6. Take safety precautions if confusion or other mental symptoms of hypercalcemia are present. Explain to the client and family that the mental changes associated with hypercalcemia are reversible with treatment. 7. Be aware that cardiac arrest can occur in clients with severe hypercalcemia; be prepared to deal with this emergency. 8. Be aware that bones may fracture more easily in clients with chronic hypercalcemia because bone resorption has been excessive, weakening the bony structure. Transfer clients cautiously. 9. Educate home-bound oncology clients with a predisposition for hypercalcemia, and their families, to be alert for symptoms that occur with this condition and to report them to the health care providers before they become severe.

10. Be alert for signs of digitalis toxicity when hypercalcemia occurs in digitalized clients.
11. Help prevent formation of calcium renal stones in clients with long-standing hypercalcemia or immobilization by:
    a. Forcing fluids to maintain a dilute urine, thus avoiding supersaturation of precipitates.
    b. Encouraging fluids that yield an acid ash (such as prune or cranberry juice) because a urinary pH <6.5 favors calcium deposits.
    c. Preventing urinary stasis by turning the immobilized client frequently, elevating the head of the bed, and having the client sit up if this can be tolerated.
    d. Encouraging weight-bearing and ambulation as soon as possible.

HYPOMAGNESEMIA

Chronic alcoholism, particularly during withdrawal

Intestinal malabsorption syndromes

Diarrhea

Nasogastric suction

Aggressive refeeding after starvation (as in TPN) without adequate magnesium replacement

Neuromuscular irritability
- Increased reflexes
- Coarse tremors
- Positive Chvostek's and Trousseau's signs
- Convulsions

1. Be aware of clients at risk for hypomagnesemia and monitor for its presence.
2. Assess digitalized clients at risk for hypomagnesemia especially closely for symptoms of digitalis toxicity because a deficit of magnesium predisposes to toxicity.
3. Be prepared to take seizure precautions when hypomagnesemia is severe.

(continued)

135

TABLE 7-4 Signs and Symptoms of Electrolyte Imbalances (Continued)

Related Factors	Defining Characteristics	Nursing Interventions
HYPOMAGNESEMIA (*cont.*)		
Prolonged administration of magnesium-free maintenance IV fluids	Cardiac manifestations	4. Monitor condition of airway, because laryngeal stridor can occur.
Diabetic ketoacidosis	• Tachyarrhythmias	5. Take safety precautions if confusion is present.
Hyperaldosteronism (either primary, or secondary, as in congestive heart failure or cirrhosis)	• Increased susceptibility to digitalis toxicity	6. Be familiar with magnesium replacement salts and factors related to their safe administration.
Drugs:	• ECG changes in severe cases: PR and QT interval prolongation, widened QRS complex, ST segment depression, and T-wave inversion	7. Be aware that magnesium-depleted clients may experience difficulty in swallowing.
• Diuretics		8. When magnesium deficit is due to abuse of diuretics or laxatives, educating the client may help alleviate the problem.
• Aminoglycoside antibiotics (eg, gentamicin)	Mental changes	9. Be aware that most commonly used IV fluids have either no magnesium or a relatively small amount. When indicated, discuss need for magnesium replacement with physician.
• Cisplatin	• Disorientation in memory	10. For clients experiencing abnormal magnesium losses, but able to consume a general diet, encourage the intake of magnesium-rich foods (such as green vegetables, nuts and legumes, and fruits such as bananas, oranges, and grapefruits).
• Excessive doses of vitamin D or calcium supplements	• Mood changes	
• Citrate preservative in blood products	• Intense confusion	
	• Hallucinations	
Pancreatitis	Serum magnesium level <1.3 mEq/L or 1.8 mg/dL (0.8 mmol/L). Usually symptoms	
Thyrotoxicosis		

Hyperparathyroidism
Others:
- Burns
- Sepsis
- Hypothermia

don't appear until serum magnesium is >1 mEq/L (0.8 mmol/L). Hypocalcemia and hypokalemia frequently occur with severe hypomagnesemia.

HYPERMAGNESEMIA

Renal failure (particularly when magnesium-containing medications are administered)

Adrenal insufficiency

Excessive magnesium administration during treatment of eclampsia

Hemodialysis with excessively hard water or with a dialysate inadvertently high in magnesium content

Untreated ketoacidosis

Early signs (serum magnesium level of 3 to 5 mEq/L)

- Flushing and a sense of skin warmth (due to peripheral vasodilation)
- Hypotension (due to blockage of sympathetic ganglia as well as to a direct effect on smooth muscle)
- Nausea and vomiting

Drowsiness, hypoactive reflexes, and muscular weakness (can occur at a serum magnesium level of 4 to 7 mEq/L)

1. Be aware of clients at risk for hypermagnesemia and assess for its presence. When hypermagnesemia is suspected, assess the following parameters:
   - Vital signs: Look for low blood pressure and shallow respirations with periods of apnea.
   - Patellar reflexes: If absent, notify physician because this usually implies a serum magnesium level >7 mEq/L. If allowed to progress, cardiac or respiratory arrest could occur.
   - Level of consciousness: Look for drowsiness, lethargy, and coma.
2. Do not give magnesium-containing medications to clients with renal failure or compromised renal function. (Be particularly careful in following "standing orders" for bowel

(continued)

TABLE 7-4 Signs and Symptoms of Electrolyte Imbalances (Continued)

Related Factors	Defining Characteristics	Nursing Interventions
HYPERMAGNESEMIA *(cont.)*		
	Depressed respirations (can occur at a serum magnesium level of 10 mEq/L)	preparation for x-ray because some of these include the use of magnesium citrate.)
	Coma (can occur at a serum magnesium level of 10 to 15 mEq/L)	3. Caution clients with renal disease to check with their health care providers before taking over-the-counter medications.
	Cardiac abnormalities	4. Be aware of factors related to safe parenteral administration of magnesium salts.
	• Sinus bradycardia, prolonged PR, QRS, and QT intervals (at serum magnesium levels of 7.1 to 10 mEq/L)	
	• Heart block and cardiac arrest in diastole (can occur at a serum magnesium level of 15 to 20 mEq/L)	
	Weak or absent cry in newborn	
HYPOPHOSPHATEMIA		
Glucose administration	Paresthesias	1. Identify clients at risk for hypophosphatemia.
Refeeding after starvation	Muscle weakness (perhaps manifested	• Particularly at risk are extremely malnourished clients

Hyperalimentation
Alcohol withdrawal
Diabetic ketoacidosis
Respiratory alkalosis
Phosphate-binding antacids
Recovery phase after severe burns

as decreased strength of hand grasp and difficulty speaking
Muscle pain and tenderness
Mental changes, such as apprehension, confusion, delirium, and coma
Cardiomyopathy
Acute respiratory failure (perhaps related to chest muscle weakness)
Seizures
Decreased tissue oxygenation
Joint stiffness
Serum phosphate <2.5 mg/dL

being started on TPN or large caloric intake by tube feeding (refeeding syndrome in starving clients).

- Also at great risk are alcoholic clients undergoing withdrawal therapy and initial treatment with intravenous fluids.
- Similarly at great risk are clients with diabetic ketoacidosis during the early treatment period with insulin and intravenous fluids.

2. Monitor clients at risk for the presence of hypophosphatemia. See *Defining Characteristics*.

3. Be aware that severely hypophosphatemic clients are thought to be at greater risk for infection because of changes in white blood cells.

4. Administer IV phosphate products cautiously. Be aware that they should be administered slowly in dilute infusion solutions to avoid phosphate intoxication. Frequent monitoring of serum phosphorus levels is required to guide therapy.

5. Be aware that in adults the usual maintenance dose of phosphorus is 10 to 15 mmol/L of TPN solution. However, maintenance doses may not be sufficient if the client is in a high anabolic state. Allowances must also be made for existing phosphorus deficit.

6. Be aware of the need to introduce hyperalimentation *gradually* in clients who are malnourished. Gradual introduction of the feeding solution is less apt to be associated with

(continued)

TABLE 7-4 Signs and Symptoms of Electrolyte Imbalances (Continued)

Related Factors	Defining Characteristics	Nursing Interventions
HYPOPHOSPHATEMIA (cont.)		
		rapid shifts of phosphate into the cells. Monitor rates of TPN flow frequently.
		7. Be aware that sudden increase in the serum phosphorus level can cause hypocalcemia. For this reason, serum calcium levels should be monitored. Watch for twitching around the mouth, laryngospasm, positive Chvostek's sign, paresthesias, arrhythmias, and hypotension.
		8. Because it is possible to give too much phosphorus when administering phosphate solutions, monitor for signs of hyperphosphatemia and of the salt in which it is administered.
		9. Monitor for diarrhea in clients taking oral phosphorus supplements; consult with physician if it persists or becomes severe.
		10. Mix powdered oral phosphorus supplements with chilled or iced water to make them more palatable. Also, palatability may be increased by refrigerating the solution made from the powder.

HYPERPHOSPHATEMIA

Renal failure

Chemotherapy, particularly for acute lymphoblastic leukemia and lymphoma

Large intake of milk, as in treatment of peptic ulcer

Use of cow's milk in infants

Excessive intake of phosphate-containing laxatives

Overzealous administration of phosphorus supplements, orally or intravenously

Excessive use of Fleet's phosphosoda as enema solution, particularly in children and people with slow bowel elimination

Large vitamin D intake (increased phosphorus absorption)

Hypoparathyroidism

Hyperthyroidism

Short-term consequences: symptoms of tetany, such as tingling of fingertips and around mouth, numbness, and muscle spasms

Long-term consequences: precipitation of calcium phosphate in nonosseous sites, such as the kidney, joints, arteries, skin, or cornea.

Serum phosphate >4.5 mg/dL

1. Identify clients at risk for hyperphosphatemia.

2. Monitor for signs of tetany, such as tingling sensations in the fingertips and around the mouth, and presence of muscle cramps or positive Chvostek's and Trousseau's signs in at-risk clients. Be aware that these symptoms are probably due to hypocalcemia induced by the high phosphate level and are most likely to occur in clients who have taken in a high phosphate load.

3. Be aware that soft-tissue calcification can be a long-term complication of a chronically elevated serum phosphate level. Calcification may occur in sites such as the kidney, arteries, joints, and cornea. Monitor for signs of these complications.

4. Administer prescribed oral and IV phosphate supplements cautiously and monitor serum phosphorus levels periodically during their use.

5. When appropriate, instruct clients that use of phosphate-containing laxatives may result in acute phosphate poisoning.

6. Be aware that phosphate-containing enemas can result in hyperphosphatemia if used injudiciously, particularly in

(continued)

141

TABLE 7-4 Signs and Symptoms of Electrolyte Imbalances (Continued)

Related Factors	Defining Characteristics	Nursing Interventions
HYPERPHOSPHATEMIA (cont.)		children and those with slow bowel emptying. Instruct clients accordingly. 7. When a low-phosphorus diet is prescribed, instruct clients to avoid foods high in phosphorus content. Such foods include hard cheese or cream, nuts and nut products; whole grain cereals (eg, bran and oatmeal); dried fruits, dried vegetables; special meats such as kidneys and sardines and sweetbreads; and desserts made with milk.

(Data from Metheny NM. Fluid and electrolyte balance, 3rd ed. Philadelphia: JB Lippincott, 1996.)

TABLE 7-5 Signs and Symptoms of Acid–Base Imbalances

Related Factors	Defining Characteristics	Nursing Interventions
RESPIRATORY ACIDOSIS (CARBONIC ACID EXCESS)		

Acute respiratory acidosis:
 	
• Acute pulmonary edema
• Aspiration of a foreign body
• Atelectasis
• Pneumothorax, hemothorax
• Overdosage of sedatives or anesthetic
• Position on operating room table that interferes with respirations
• Cardiac arrest
• Severe pneumonia
• Laryngospasm
• Mechanical ventilation improperly regulated
 	
Chronic respiratory acidosis:
 	
• Emphysema
• Cystic fibrosis
• Advanced multiple sclerosis
	Acute respiratory acidosis
	
	• Feeling of fullness in the head ($Paco_2$ causes cerebrovascular vasodilation and increased cerebral blood flow, particularly when >60 mm Hg)
	• Mental cloudiness
	• Dizziness
	• Palpitations
	• Muscular twitching
	• Convulsions
	• Warm, flushed skin
	• Unconsciousness
	• Ventricular fibrillation may be first sign in anesthetized patient (related to hyperkalemia)
	• Arterial blood gases (ABGs)
	
	  • ph <7.35
	  • $Paco_2$ >45 mm Hg (primary)
		Treatment is directed at improving ventilation; exact measures vary with the cause of inadequate ventilation. Pharmacologic agents are used as indicated. For example, bronchodilators help reduce bronchial spasm; antibiotics are used for respiratory infections. Pulmonary hygiene measures are used, when necessary, to rid the respiratory tract of mucus and purulent drainage. Adequate hydration (2 to 3 L/day) is indicated to keep the mucous membranes moist and thereby facilitate removal of secretions. Supplemental oxygen is used as necessary.
		
		A mechanical respirator, used cautiously, may improve pulmonary ventilation. One must remember that overzealous use of a mechanical respirator may cause such rapid excretion of carbon dioxide that the kidneys
		                      (continued)

143

TABLE 7-5 Signs and Symptoms of Acid–Base Imbalances (Continued)

Related Factors	Defining Characteristics	Nursing Interventions
RESPIRATORY ACIDOSIS (CARBONIC ACID EXCESS) *(cont.)*		
Chronic respiratory acidosis *(cont.)*	• HCO_3^- normal or only slightly elevated	will be unable to eliminate excess bicarbonate with sufficient rapidity to prevent alkalosis and convulsions. For this reason, the elevated $Paco_2$ must be decreased slowly.
• Bronchiectasis		
• Bronchial asthma	Chronic respiratory acidosis	
Factors favoring hypoventilation:	• Weakness	
	• Dull headache	
• Obesity	• Symptoms of underlying disease process	
• Tight abdominal binders or dressings	• ABGs	
• Postoperative pain (as in high abdominal or chest incisions	• pH <7.35 or within lower limits of normal	
• Abdominal distention from cirrhosis or bowel obstruction	• $Paco_2$ >45 mm Hg (primary)	
	• HCO_3^- >26 mEq/L (mmol/L) (compensatory)	
RESPIRATORY ALKALOSIS (CARBONIC ACID DEFICIT)		
Extreme anxiety (most common cause)	Lightheadedness (a low $Paco_2$ causes cerebral vasoconstriction and thus decreased cerebral blood flow)	If the cause of respiratory alkalosis is anxiety, the client should be made aware that the abnormal breathing practice is responsible
Hypoxemia		
High fever		

Early salicylate intoxication (stimulates respiratory center)

Gram-negative bacteremia

Central nervous system lesions involving respiratory center

Pulmonary emboli

Thyrotoxicosis

Excessive ventilation by mechanical ventilators

Pregnancy (high progesterone level sensitizes the respiratory center to CO_2; physiologic)

Inability to concentrate

Those of decreased calcium ionization (numbness and tingling of extremities and circumoral paresthesia; more likely to occur if respiratory alkalosis develops rapidly)

Hyperventilation syndrome

- Tinnitus
- Palpitations
- Sweating
- Dry mouth
- Tremulousness
- Precordial pain (tightness)
- Nausea and vomiting
- Epigastric pain
- Blurred vision
- Convulsions and loss of consciousness (may be partly due to cerebral ischemia, caused by cerebral vasoconstriction)

ABGs

- pH >7.45
- $Paco_2$ <35 mm Hg (primary)
- Hco_3^- <22 mEq/L (mmol/L) (compensatory)

for the symptoms accompanying this condition. Instructing the client to breathe more slowly (to cause accumulation of carbon dioxide) or to breathe in a closed system (such as a paper bag) is helpful. Usually a sedative is required to relieve ventilation in very anxious patients. (If alkalosis is severe enough to cause fainting, the increased ventilation ceases and respirations revert to normal.)

Treatment for other causes of respiratory alkalosis is directed at correcting the underlying problem.

(continued)

145

TABLE 7-5 Signs and Symptoms of Acid–Base Imbalances (Continued)

Related Factors	Defining Characteristics	Nursing Interventions
METABOLIC ACIDOSIS (BASE BICARBONATE DEFICIT)		

Normal anion gap:
• Diarrhea
• Intestinal fistulas
• Ureterosigmoidostomy
• Hyperalimentation
• Acidifying drugs (eg, ammonium chloride)
• Renal tubular acidosis (RTA)
 	
High anion gap:
• Diabetic ketoacidosis
• Starvational ketoacidosis
• Lactic acidosis
• Renal failure
• Ingestion of toxins (eg, salicylates, ethylene glycol, and methanol)
	Headache
	Confusion
	Drowsiness
	Increased respiratory rate and depth (may not become clinically evident until HCO_3^- is quite low)
	Nausea and vomiting
	Peripheral vasodilation (may be present, causing warm, flushed skin)
	Decreased cardiac output when pH falls below 7; bradycardia may develop
	ABGs
	  • Fall in pH to <7.35
	  • HCO_3^- <22 mEq/L (mmol/L) (primary)
	  • $PaCO_2$ <35 mm Hg (compensation by lungs)
	  • Base excess always negative
	Hyperkalemia is frequently present (except in RTA, diarrhea, and use of acetazolamide)
		Treatment is directed toward correcting the metabolic defect. If the cause of the problem is excessive intake of chloride, treatment obviously focuses on eliminating the source. When necessary, bicarbonate is administered.

METABOLIC ALKALOSIS (BASE BICARBONATE EXCESS)

Vomiting or gastric suction

Hypokalemia

Hyperaldosteronism

Cushing's syndrome

Potassium-losing diuretics (eg, thiazides, furosemide, ethacrynic acid)

Alkali ingestion (bicarbonate-containing antacids)

Parenteral NaHCO₃ administration for cardiopulmonary resuscitation

Abrupt relief of chronic respiratory acidosis

Those related to decreased calcium ionization, such as:

- Dizziness
- Tingling of fingers and toes
- Circumoral paresthesia
- Carpopedal spasm
- Hypertonic muscles

Depressed respiration (compensatory action by lungs)

ABGs

- pH >7.45
- Bicarbonate >26 mEq/L (mmol/L) (primary)
- Paco₂ >45 mm Hg (compensatory)
- Base excess always positive

Hypokalemia often present

Serum Cl relatively lower than Na

Treatmexnt is aimed at reversal of the underlying disorder. Sufficient chloride must be supplied for the kidney to absorb sodium with chloride (allowing the excretion of excess bicarbonate). Treatment also includes restoration of normal fluid volume by administration of sodium chloride fluids (because continued volume depletion serves to maintain the alkalosis).

(Data from Metheny NM. Fluid and electrolyte balance, 3rd ed. Philadelphia: JB Lippincott, 1996.)

TABLE 7-6 Signs and Symptoms of Water Excess or Deficit

Site	Hyponatremia (Water Intoxication)	Hypernatremia (Water Deficit)
CNS	Muscle twitching	Restlessness
	Hyperactive tendon reflexes	Weakness
	Convulsions	Delirium
	Increased intracranial pressure, coma	Coma
CV	Increased BP and pulse, if severe	Tachycardia
		Hypotension (if severe)
Tissues	Increased salivation, tears	Decreased saliva and tears
	Watery diarrhea	Dry, sticky mucous membranes
	Fingerprinting of skin	Red, swollen tongue
		Flushed skin
Renal	Oliguria	Oliguria
Other	None	Fever

TABLE 7-7 Signs and Symptoms of Isotonic Fluid Excess or Deficit

Site	Deficit	Excess
CNS	Fatigue, apathy	Confusion (if severe)
	Anorexia	
	Stupor, coma	
CV	Orthostatic hypotension	Elevated venous pressure
	Flat neck veins	Distended neck veins
	Fast, thready pulse	Increased cardiac output
	Hypotension	Heart gallops
	Cool, clammy skin	Pulmonary edema
GI	Anorexia	Anorexia, nausea, and vomiting
	Thirst	Edema of stomach, colon, and mesentery
	Silent ileus	
Tissues	Soft, small tongue with longitudinal wrinkling	Pitting edema
	Sunken eyes	Moist pulmonary crackles
	Decreased skin turgor	
Metabolism	Mild decrease in temperature	None

CHAPTER 8

Renal and Urologic Reference Facts

TABLE 8-1 Normal Urine Characteristics

Characteristic	Normal Findings	Special Considerations
Color	A freshly voided specimen is pale yellow, straw-colored, or amber, depending on its concentration.	Urine is darker than normal when it is scanty and concentrated. Urine is lighter than normal when it is excessive and diluted. Certain drugs, such as cascara, L-dopa, and sulfonamides, alter the color of urine.
Odor	Normal urine is aromatic. As urine stands, it often develops an ammonia odor because of bacterial action.	Some foods cause urine to have a characteristic odor; for example, asparagus causes urine to have a strong, musty odor. Urine high in glucose content has a sweet odor. Urine that is heavily infected has a fetid odor.
Turbidity	Fresh urine should be clear or translucent; as urine stands and cools, it becomes cloudy.	Cloudiness observed in freshly voided urine is abnormal and may be due to the presence of red blood cells, white blood cells, bacteria, vaginal discharge, sperm, or prostatic fluid.

(continued)

TABLE 8-1 Normal Urine Characteristics (Continued)

Characteristic	Normal Findings	Special Considerations
pH	The normal pH is about 6.0, with a range of 4.6 to 8. (Urine alkalinity or acidity may be promoted through diet to inhibit bacterial growth or urinary stone development or to facilitate the therapeutic activity of certain medications.) Urine becomes alkaline on standing when carbon dioxide diffuses into the air.	A high-protein diet causes urine to become excessively acidic. Certain foods tend to produce alkaline urine, such as citrus fruits, dairy products, and vegetables, especially legumes. Certain foods tend to produce acidic urine, for example, meat and cranberry juice. Certain drugs influence the acidity or alkalinity of urine; for example, ammonium chloride produces acidic urine, and potassium citrate and sodium bicarbonate produce alkaline urine.
Specific gravity	This is a measure of the concentration of dissolved solids in the urine. The normal range is 1.010 to 1.025.	Concentrated urine has a higher than normal specific gravity and diluted urine has a lower than normal specific gravity. In the absence of kidney disease, a high specific gravity usually indicates dehydration and a low specific gravity indicates overhydration.
Constituents	*Organic* constituents of urine include urea, uric acid, creatinine, hippuric acid, indican, urene pigments, and undetermined nitrogen. *Inorganic* constituents are ammonia, sodium, chloride, traces of iron, phosphorus, sulfur, potassium, and calcium.	*Abnormal constituents* of urine include blood, pus, albumin, glucose, ketone bodies, casts, gross bacteria, and bile.

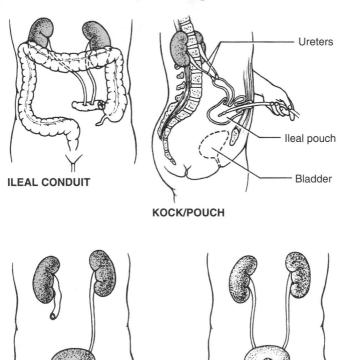

ILEAL CONDUIT

Ureters

Ileal pouch

Bladder

KOCK/POUCH

URETEROSTOMY

VESICOSTOMY

FIGURE 8-1 Urinary diversions.

TABLE 8-2 Renal Function Tests

1. There is no single test of renal function; renal function is variable from time to time.
2. The rate of change of renal function is more important than the result of a single test.

Test	Purpose/Rationale	Test Protocol
Renal concentration test Specific gravity Osmolality of urine	Tests the ability to concentrate solutes in the urine Concentration ability is lost early in kidney disease; hence, this test detects early defects in renal function.	Fluids may be withheld 12–24 h to evaluate the concentrating ability of the tubules under controlled conditions. Specific gravity measurements of urine are taken at specific times to determine urine concentration.
Creatinine clearance	Provides a reasonable approximation of rate of glomerular filtration Measures volume of blood cleared of creatinine in 1 min Most sensitive indication of early renal disease Useful to follow progress of the patient's renal status	Collect all urine over 24-h period. Draw one sample of blood within the period.

Serum creatinine	A test of renal function reflecting the balance between production and filtration by renal glomerulus. Most sensitive test of renal function	Do test on blood serum.
Serum urea nitrogen (blood urea nitrogen [BUN])	Serves as index of renal excretory capacity. Serum urea nitrogen depends on the body's urea production and on urine flow. (Urea is the nitrogenous end-product of protein metabolism.) Affected by protein intake, tissue breakdown	Do test on blood serum.
Protein	Random specimen may be affected by dietary protein intake. Proteinuria >150 mg/24 h may indicate renal disease.	Collect all urine over 24-h period.
Urine casts	Mucoproteins and other substances present in renal inflammation; help to identify type of renal disease (eg, red cell casts present in glomerulonephritis, fatty casts in nephrotic syndrome, white cell casts in pyelonephritis)	Collect random urine specimen.

TABLE 8-3 Categories of Renal Failure

PRERENAL FAILURE

Dehydration
Sepsis/shock
Hypovolemic shock
Vena cava obstruction
Trauma with bleeding
Sequestration (burns, peritonitis)
Hypovolemia (eg, diuretics)
Cardiovascular failure (eg, myocardial failure, tamponade, vascular pooling, congestive heart failure, dysrhythmia)
Hemorrhage
Gastrointestinal losses (diarrhea, vomiting)
Extreme acidosis
Anaphylaxis/shock
Renal artery stenosis or thrombosis

INTRARENAL FAILURE

Acute glomerulonephritis
Severe renal ischemia
Chemicals (eg, radiographics dyes, commercial chemicals)
Certain drugs (eg, anti-inflammatory drugs, antibiotics)
Neoplasms
Malignant hypertension
Systemic lupus erythematosus
Diabetes mellitus
Complications of pregnancy (eg, eclampsia)
Streptococcal infections
Vasopressors
Microangiopathy
Hyperviscosity states
Hypercalcemia
Postrenal transplant
Myeloma
Interstitial nephritis
Transfusion reactions
HIV nephropathy
Heroin nephropathy

TABLE 8-3 Categories of Renal Failure (Continued)

●●●

POSTRENAL FAILURE

Kidney stones
Clots
Structure malformation
Tumors
Prostatitism
Rupture of the bladder
Ureteral obstruction
Retroperitoneal fibrosis
Bilateral renal venous occlusion
Neurogenic bladder

●●●

TABLE 8-4 Recommended Antibiotic Dosage in Renal Failure

		Adjustment for Renal Failure			
		GFR (mL/min)			
Antibiotic Group	Method	>50	10–50	<10	Dialysis Supplement
Aminoglycosides	I*	12–18	12	24	Yes
Amikacin					
Gentamicin					
Kanamicin					
Netilmicin					
Streptomycin					
Tobramicin					
Cephalosporins					Yes
All except Cefoperazone require reduction, but adjustments vary significantly between drugs.					
Cefaclor	D†	100	50–100	33	Yes
Cefadroxil	I	8	12–24	24–48	Yes
Cefamandole	I	6	6–8	8	Yes
Cefazolin	I	8	12	24–48	Yes
Cefoperazone	I	—	None‡	—	Yes

Ceforanide	I	12	24–48	48–72	Yes
Cefotaximine	I	6–8	8–12	12–24	Yes
Cefoxitin	I	8	8–12	24–48	Yes
Cefroxadine	D	65–100	15–65	10–15	?
Cefuroxime	I	8–12	24–48	48–72	Yes
Cefsulodin	D	50–100	15–50	10–15	Yes
Ceftizoxime	D	45–100	10–45	5–10	?
Cephalothin	I	6	6	8–12	Yes
Cephalexin	I	6	6–8	12	Yes
Cephapirin	I	6	6–8	12	Yes
Cephradrine	D	100	50	25	Yes
Moxalactam	I	8	12	12–24	Yes
Clindamycin	D	—	None	—	Yes
Erythromycin	D	—	None	—	Yes
Lincomycin	I	6	12	24	Yes
Methenanime mandelate	D	100	Avoid§	Avoid	—
Nalidixic acid	D	100	Avoid	Avoid	—
Nitrofurantoin	D	100	Avoid	Avoid	—
Penicillins					
Amoxicillin	I	6	6–12	12–16	Yes
Ampicillin	I	6	6–12	12–16	Yes
Azlocillin	I	4–6	6–8	8	Yes
Carbenicillin	I	8–12	12–24	24–48	Yes
Cloxacillin	D	—	None	—	No‖

(continued)

TABLE 8-4 Recommended Antibiotic Dosage in Renal Failure (Continued)

		Adjustment for Renal Failure			
			GFR (mL/min)		
Antibiotic Group	Method	>50	10–50	<10	Dialysis Supplement
Cyclacillin	I	6	6–12	12–24	Yes
Dicloxacillin	I	—	None	—	No
Methicillin	I	4	4–8	8–12	No
Mezlocillin	I	4–6	6–8	8	Yes
Nafcillin	D	—	None	—	No
Oxacillin	D	—	None	—	No
Penicillin G	I	6–8	8–12	12–16	Yes
Piperacillin	I	4–6	6–8	8	Yes
Ticarcillin	I	8–12	12–24	24–48	Yes

Sulfonamides and trimethoprim					
Sulfamethoxazole	I	12	18	24	Yes
Sulfisoxazole	I	6	8–12	12–24	Yes
Trimethoprim	I	12	18	24	Yes
Tetracyclines					
Doxycycline	I	12	12–18	18–24	No
Minocycline	D	—	None	—	No
Vancomycin	I	24–72	72–240	240	No

* *I* Refers to alteration in dosage interval in hours.

† *D* refers to percentage of alteration of usual dose.

‡ *None* means no dosage adjustment is necessary.

§ *Avoid* means drugs toxic in renal failure.

‖ *No* means that hemodialysis does not significantly alter kinetics of the drug.

Modified from Bennett WM, et al. Drug prescribing in renal failure: Dosing guidelines for adults. Am J Kidney Dis 3:155–193, 1983.

TABLE 8-5 Routine Urinalysis*

General Characteristics and Measurements	Chemical Determinations	Microscopic Examination of Sediment
Color: pale yellow to amber	Glucose: negative	Casts negative: occasional hyaline casts
Appearance: clear to slightly hazy	Ketones: negative	Red blood cells: negative or rare
Specific gravity: 1.015–1.025 with a normal fluid intake	Blood: negative	Crystals: negative
pH: 4.5–8.0—average person has a pH of about 5–6	Protein: negative	White blood cells: negative or rare
Volume: 1500/24 h	Bilirubin: negative Urobilinogen: 0.1–1.0 Nitrate for bacteria: negative Leukocyte esterase: negative	Epithelial cells: few

* Normal values

TABLE 8-6 24-Hour Urine Collection Data

Test	Preservative	Protocols
Acid mucopolysaccharides	20 mL toluene	Add at start of collection
Aldosterone	1 g boric acid/100 mL urine	
Amylase	None	Refrigerate during collection
Arsenic	None	Refrigerate during collection
Cadmium	None	Refrigerate during collection
Calcium	None	Refrigerate during collection
Catecholamines	20 mL 8 N* acetic acid	Refrigerate during collection
Chloride	None	Refrigerate during collection
Copper	None	Refrigerate during collection
Cortisol (free)	None	Refrigerate during collection
Creatinine	None	Refrigerate during collection
Creatinine clearance	None	Refrigerate during collection
Cyclic AMP	None	Refrigerate during collection
Cystine	None	Refrigerate during collection

TABLE 8-6 24-Hour Urine Collection
Data (Continued)
• •

Test	Preservative	Protocols
Δ-Aminolevulinic acid (ALA)	1 mL of 33% glacial acetic acid/10 mL urine	Refrigerate during collection
Electrolytes Na	None	Refrigerate during collection
Estrogens	None	Refrigerate during collection
5-HIAA (serotonin)	1 g boric acid	Refrigerate during collection
Histamine	None	Freeze portion after collection
Homogentisic acid	None	Freeze portion after collection
Hydroxyproline	None	
FSH/LH	1 g boric acid	
17-Hydroxycorticosteroids	1 g boric acid	Do not refrigerate
17-Ketogenic steroid (Porter-Silber)	1 g boric acid	Do not refrigerate
17-Ketosteroids (total)	1 g boric acid	Do not refrigerate
Magnesium	None	
Metanephrine (total)	2 mL acetic acid	
Oxalate	None	Refrigerate during collection
Phosphorus (inorganic)	None	Refrigerate during collection
Pregnanediol	None	Refrigerate during collection
Protein (total)	*See* Total Protein	Refrigerate during collection
Porphobilinogens	None	Refrigerate during collection; protect from light
Potassium (K), sodium (Na)	None	Refrigerate during collection
Porphyrins (uro/copro)	None (preservative added on receipt in lab)	Refrigerate during collection; protect from light
Thiocyanate	None	Refrigerate during collection
Total protein	None	Refrigerate during collection
Urea nitrogen	None	Refrigerate during collection
Uric acid	None	Refrigerate during collection
Vanillylmandelic acid (VMA)	20 mL SN acetic acid before collection	

• •

* N = normal.

TABLE 8-7 Blood Urea Nitrogen (BUN)*

Child:	5–18 mg/dL, or 1.8–6.4 mmol/L
Adult:	7–18 mg/dL, or 2.5–6.4 mmol/L
>60 y:	8–20 mg/dL, or 2.9–7.5 mmol/L

* Normal values.

CHAPTER 9

Endocrine and Metabolic Reference Facts

TABLE 9-1 Clinical Manifestations of Endocrine Dysfunction
••

Body System	Signs or Symptoms	Possible Causes
Cardiovascular	Tachycardia or tachyarrhythmia	Hyperthyroidism, pheochromocytoma
		Adrenal insufficiency
	Bradycardia	Hypothyroidism
	Orthostatic hypotension	Adrenal insufficiency
		Hyperaldosteronism
		Pheochromocytoma
	Hypertension	Pheochromocytoma
		Hyperaldosteronism
		Cushing's syndrome
		Hyperparathyroidism
		Hypothyroidism
	Heart failure	Hyperthyroidism
		Hypothyroidism
		Cushing's syndrome
Neurologic	Fatigue	Adrenal insufficiency
		Hypothyroidism
		Hyperparathyroidism
	Nervousness, tremor	Pheochromocytoma
		Hyperthyroidism
	Confusion, lethargy, or coma	Diabetic ketoacidosis
		Hypothyroidism
		Syndrome of inappropriate antidiuretic hormone (SIADH)
	Paresthesia	Hypothyroidism
		Hypoparathyroidism
		Diabetes mellitus
	Headache	Acromegaly
		Pituitary tumor
		Pheochromocytoma
	Psychosis	Hyperaldosteronism
		Hypothyroidism
		Hyperthyroidism
		Cushing's syndrome
		Adrenal insufficiency
		Hyperparathyroidism

(continued)

TABLE 9-1 Clinical Manifestations of Endocrine Dysfunction (Continued)

Body System	Signs or Symptoms	Possible Causes
Neurologic (cont.)	Chvostek's sign, Trousseau's sign	Syndrome of inappropriate antidiuretic hormone (SIADH)
	Increased reflexes	Hypoparathyroidism
	Decreased reflexes	Hyperthyroidism
		Hypothyroidism
Gastrointestinal	Anorexia	Addison's disease
		Hypothyroidism
		Hyperparathyroidism
	Peptic ulcer	Cushing's syndrome
	Diarrhea	Adrenal insufficiency
	Constipation	Hypothyroidism
		Hyperparathyroidism
		Pheochromocytoma
	Weight loss	Hyperthyroidism
		Hyperparathyroidism
		Pheochromocytoma
		Diabetes insipidus
	Hyperdefecation	Hyperthyroidism
	Abdominal pain	Addison's crisis
		Hyperparathyroidism
		Thyroid storm
		Myxedema
Musculoskeletal	Weakness	Hyperthyroidism
		Hypothyroidism
		Cushing's syndrome
		Adrenal insufficiency
		Hyperparathyroidism
		Hypoparathyroidism
		Hyperaldosteronism
	Pathologic fractures	Hyperparathyroidism
	Joint pain	Hypothyroidism
		Acromegaly
	Bone pain	Hyperparathyroidism
	Bone thickening	Acromegaly
Urologic	Polyuria	Hyperparathyroidism
		Diabetes insipidus
		Diabetes mellitus
		Hyperaldosteronism

**TABLE 9-1 Clinical Manifestations of
Endocrine Dysfunction** (Continued)

Body System	Signs or Symptoms	Possible Causes
Urologic (cont.)	Kidney stones	Hyperparathyroidism Acromegaly Cushing's syndrome
Integumentary	Hirsutism	Adrenal hyperfunction Acromegaly
	Hair loss	Hypoparathyroidism Hypothyroidism Cushing's syndrome
	Sparse body hair	Pituitary insufficiency Adrenal insufficiency Hypogonadism
	Hyperpigmentation	Addison's disease Hyperthyroidism Ectopic corticotropin production
	Profuse diaphoresis	Hyperthyroidism Pheochromocytoma
	Fine skin	Cushing's syndrome
	Coarse hair	Hypothyroidism
	Fine hair	Hyperthyroidism
	Edema	Cushing's syndrome
Reproductive	Amenorrhea	Hyperthyroidism Hypogonadism Cushing's syndrome Acromegaly Pituitary tumor
	Gynecomastia	Hypogonadism Pituitary tumor
	Loss of libido, impotence	Hypogonadism Hypothyroidism Adrenal insufficiency Diabetes mellitus
Ophthalmic/Visual	Exophthalmos	Graves' disease
	Diplopia	Graves' disease Pituitary tumor
	Visual field deficit	Pituitary tumor
	Periorbital swelling	Hypothyroidism Graves' disease
Body habitus	Round face, "buffalo hump"	Cushing's syndrome
	Abnormally tall stature	Prepubertal growth Hormone excess

TABLE 9-2 International Classification of Diabetes and Other Glucose Intolerance*

Five Major Clinical Classes					Two Statistical Classes	
Type 1	Type 2	Type 3	Type 4	Type 5	No. 1	No. 2
Insulin-dependent diabetes mellitus (IDDM)	Non–insulin-dependent diabetes mellitus (NIDDM) A. Nonobese B. Obese	Diabetes mellitus with other conditions or syndromes	Impaired glucose tolerance (IGT) A. Nonobese B. Obese C. Associated with other diseases or conditions	Gestational diabetes (GDM)	Previous abnormality of glucose tolerance (Prev AGT)	Potential abnormality of glucose tolerance (Pot AGT)

Diagnostic Criteria

Types 1 & 2	Type 3	Type 4	Type 5	Nos. 1 & 2
Adults		Adults		Adults
Classic symptoms and unequivocal elevation of plasma glucose or	Same as for IDDM including associated conditions	Fasting plasma glucose <140 mg/dL; oral	Two of the following minimum levels: Fasting plasma	Fasting plasma glucose <115 mg/dL; oral glucose tolerance test <200 mg/dL at 1 h, <140

Fasting plasma glucose >140 mg/dL more than once

or

Oral glucose tolerance test (challenge dose 75 g) >200 mg/dL at 1 and 2 h, confirmed by repetition.

or syndromes

glucose tolerance test >200 mg/dL at 1 h; 140–199 mg/dL at 2 h

glucose >105 mg/dL; oral glucose tolerance test (challenge dose 100 g) >190 mg/dL at 1 h, >165 mg/dL at 2 h, or >145 mg/dL at 3 h

mg/dL at 2 h

Children

Fasting plasma glucose <140 mg/dL; oral glucose tolerance test >140 mg/dL at 2 h

Children

Fasting plasma glucose <130 mg/dL; oral glucose tolerance <140 mg/dL at 2 h

Children

Classic symptoms and random plasma glucose >200 mg/dL

or

Fasting plasma glucose >140 mg/dL more than once

and

Oral glucose tolerance test (challenge dose 1.75 g/kg ideal body weight, up to a maximum of 75 g) >200 mg/dL at 1 and 2 h, confirmed by repetition.

* National Diabetes Data Group, National Institutes of Health, Bethesda, MD.

171

TABLE 9-3 Chronic Complications of Diabetes Mellitus

Condition	Assessment	Intervention
MACROANGIOPATHY		
Cerebrovascular Disease		
Incidence: Twice as frequent in diabetes Hypertension, increased lipids, smoking, and uncontrolled blood glucose, increased risk of stroke and transient ischemic attack.	Increased blood pressure Change in mental status Hemiparesis Aphasia Clinical presentation mimics that of nondiabetic patient	Check blood glucose level to differentiate s/s of stroke vs. hypoglycemia. If stroke is suspected, do *not* give fast-acting carbohydrate as increased levels contribute to recurrence and ↑ mortality rates of strokes in patients with diabetes.
Coronary Artery Disease		
Incidence: Increased vessel disease with more vessels affected in diabetes. Higher incidence of "silent" myocardial infarctions. Hyperglycemia contributes to atherosclerosis and vessel deterioration.	Severe coronary artery disease is often asymptomatic, seen only in ECG changes. ECG changes may indicate silent myocardial infarction. Symptoms can also present as pain in the jaw, neck, or epigastric area.	Usual medical treatment for angina prevails— sublingual nitroglycerin, oral nitrates. β-Adrenergic blockers and calcium channel blockers can also be used.

Peripheral Vascular Disease

Incidence: 50% of nontraumatic amputations are related to diabetes.

Intermittent claudication, absent pedal pulses, and ischemic gangrene are increased in diabetes.

Physical examination of the lower extremities may reveal changes in skin integrity associated with diminished circulation.

Decreased lower leg hair, absent or decreased anterior tibial or dorsal pedis pulses, poor capillary refill of toenails may occur. The extremity may appear pale/cool. Further examination for neurologic changes is indicated.

Any lesion, decrease in peripheral pulses, or change in skin color, temperature or sensation should be evaluated within 24–48 h. To ensure proper healing and prevent infection, treatment should begin as soon as possible and be carefully monitored. Mild antiseptics/antibiotic preparations are used to avoid further damage to the surrounding skin. Avoid the use of surgical tape on skin. Elevate affected leg to promote circulation and wound healing.

MICROANGIOPATHY
Retinopathy

Incidence: Type I—10 y postdiagnosis 60% have some degree of retinopathy. Type II—approximately 20% present with retinopathy at diagnosis, which increases to 60–85% after 15 y.

Appearance of hard exudates, blot hemorrhages, and microaneurysms on the retina in background retinopathy.

Usually asymptomatic in the early stages. Symptoms occurring with acute visual problems—"floaters," flashing lights, blurred vision—may indicate hemorrhage or retinal detachment. Funduscopic examination should be done by an ophthalmologist for full retinal visualization.

Laser therapy (photocoagulation) can be helpful in macular edema (focal laser) and proliferative retinopathy (panretinal laser). Reduction of active neovascularization by laser therapy reduces the risk of vitreous hemorrhage. Vitrectomy may be needed to treat retinal detachment or remove vitreous hemorrhage.

(continued)

173

TABLE 9-3 Chronic Complications of Diabetes Mellitus (Continued)

Condition	Assessment	Intervention
MICROANGIOPATHY (cont.)		
Retinopathy (cont.)		
Progresses to neurovascularization in proliferative diabetic retinopathy.		During the acute phase, before laser therapy, patients must avoid activities that increase the chances of vitreous hemorrhage (eg, weight lifting, high-impact aerobics).
Nephropathy		
Incidence: Type 1—with >20 y history of diabetes, approximately 40% will have renal disease. Type II—5–10 y after diagnosis 5–10% of patients develop nephropathy, with higher incidence in Native Americans, Hispanics, and African Americans. Thickening of the glomerular basement membrane, mesangial expansion, and renal vessel sclerosis are caused by diabetes. Subsequently, diffuse and nodular inter-capillary glomerulosclerosis diminishes renal function.	Evidence of ↑ glomerular filtration rate. Microalbuminuria is the first clinical sign of renal disease. Elevation in BUN and creatinine indicates advanced renal disease. Gross proteinuria is further indication of renal deterioration.	Hypertension control, blood glucose control, and protein and sodium reduction are essential. Angiotensin-converting enzyme inhibitors and calcium channel blockers are the drugs of choice to control blood pressure. In end-stage renal disease dialysis or transplantation may be necessary.

PERIPHERAL NEUROPATHY

In general, neuropathy affects 60% of persons with diabetes, with nearly 100% showing signs and symptoms of slowing nerve conduction velocity.

It can affect almost every organ system with varying specific symptoms.

Distal symmetrical polyneuropathy involving the lower extremities is most commonly seen.

In conjunction with peripheral vascular disease, neuropathy to the feet increases susceptibility to trauma and infection.

Three clinical syndromes of distal symmetrical polyneuropathy can be seen: acute painful neuropathy, small-fiber neuropathy, large-fiber neuropathy.

Decreased light touch, vibratory, temperature sensation. Loss of foot proprioception, followed by ataxia, gait disturbances.

Diminished ankle jerk response.

Formation of "hammer toes;" Charcot joint disease, which predispose patient to new pressure point areas.

Hypersensitivity or other dysesthetic symptoms are experienced, followed by hypoesthesis or anesthesia, which is not reversible.

All foot wounds or injuries are immediately evaluated. Culture and sensitivities are ordered for any drainage present. Affected foot is elevated—avoid weight-bearing. Wet to dry dressings applied as ordered. Avoid use of caustic chemicals, dressing tapes.

Use of systemic antibiotics as needed.

Medication for painful neuropathy may include use of the tricyclic antidepressant drugs (eg, amitriptylline, Elavil) or topical application of capsaicin (Zostrix) ointment.

AUTONOMIC NEUROPATHY

Gastroparesis

Incidence: Occurs in 25% of people with diabetes

Characteristics: Delayed gastric emptying,

Typical symptoms may include:

Nausea/vomiting, early satiety, abdominal bloating, epigastric pain, change in appetite.

Excellent glucose control to avoid hyperglycemia, which interferes with gut contractility. Avoidance of severe postmeal hypo-

(continued)

175

TABLE 9-3 Chronic Complications of Diabetes Mellitus (Continued)

Condition	Assessment	Intervention
AUTONOMIC NEUROPATHY (cont.)		
Gastroparesis (cont.)		
prolonged pylorospasms, and loss of the powerful contractions of the distal stomach to grind and mix foods.	Wide fluctuations in blood glucoses and postmeal hypoglycemia caused by poor glucose absorption. Visualization of the gut by upper gastrointestinal barium series may show retained food after an 8–12 h fast.	glycemia by small frequent meals, low fat and low fiber. This diet is also helpful in bloating/early satiety. Medications to improve gut motility include: metoclopramide (Reglan) and cisapride (Pepcid).
Diarrhea		
Incidence: Approximately 5% of diabetic patients Characteristics: Frequent, watery movements Mild steatorrhea Can be intermittent, persistent, or alternate with constipation.	Diarrhea occurs without warning, frequently at night or after meals. Fecal incontinence may be caused by loss of internal sphincter control and anorectal sensation. Other causes such as celiac sprue, pancreatic insufficiency, lactose intolerance must be investigated. Bacterial overgrowth in the bowel is also suspected.	Dietary changes may include: increased fiber, elimination of milk products. Sphincter-strengthening exercises may help. Medications: For diarrhea hydrophilic fiber supplement (Metamucil), cholestyramine (Questran), or synthetic opiates are used. Tetracycline, ampicillin are used for bacterial overgrowth.

Impotence/Sexual Dysfunction

Incidence is not well documented due to inhibitions about reporting this problem to health care providers.

Sexual dysfunction can involve changes in erectile ability, ejaculation, or libido.

Men: History of poor erectile function despite stimulation. Absence of early morning erection in response to increased hormonal levels.

Women: May experience decreased vaginal lubrication and dyspareunia.

Screening for use of ethanol or other medications associated with impotence (eg, antidepressants, antihypertensives).

Men: Referral to urologist for full examination is indicated. Treatment options may include papaverine (Pavased) injections, noninvasive devices for promoting and maintaining erections, or semirigid or inflatable penile prosthesis.

Women: Increase lubrication with use of water-based lubricant (K-Y jelly) or estrogen creams, which also may help thicken the vaginal mucosa, affecting dyspareunia.

Orthostatic Hypotension

One of three syndromes associated with cardiovascular autonomic neuropathy, orthostatic hypotension occurs when the "postural reflex," which increases heart rate and peripheral vascular resistance, is dysfunctional.

Patients may report episodes of syncope, weakness, or visual impairment, particularly with positional changes. Evaluate blood pressure and pulse in both supine and standing position at each visit. Blood pressure changes that indicate neuropathic involvement: fall in systolic pressure of >30 mm Hg or fall in diastolic pressure of >10 mm Hg with change from supine to standing position.

Improvement in blood glucose control to prevent fluid loss from glycosuria. Moderate amounts of sodium may be used in the diet to encourage fluid retention during hot weather or strenuous exercise. Mechanical devices such as support stockings (full hose to waist) may decrease venous pooling. Drugs to enhance volume expansion may be used (eg, fludrocortisone—Florinef).

TABLE 9-4 Insulin

Type	Product*
RAPID-ACTING	
Onset 5–15 min	Lispro (Humalog [L])
Peak 30–90 min	
Duration <5 h	
SHORT-ACTING	
Onset 0.25–1 h	Regular (L, NN)[†]
Peak 2–4 h	Velosulin (NN)
Duration 5–7 h	Humulin R (L)
	Novolin R (NN)
	Iletin II regular (L)
	Semilente (NN)
	Purified pork regular (NN)
	Iletin I regular (L)
	Iletin I semilente (L)
	Humulin BR (L)
	Velosulin Human R (NN)
INTERMEDIATE-ACTING	
Onset 1–4 h	Semilente (L, NN)
Peak 2–15 h	Semitard (NN)
Duration 12–24 h	Protaphane NPH (NN)
	NPH (L, NN)
	Monotard (NN)
	Insulatard (NN)
	Lente (L, NN)
	Lentard (NN)
	Humulin (L)
	Novulin N (NN)
	Iletin II lente (L)
	Iletin II NPH (L)
	Purified pork regular (NN)
	Purified pork NPH (NN)
	Insulatard NPH (NN)
	Iletin I NPH (L)
	Iletin I lente (L)
	Humulin L (lente) (L)
	Humulin N (NPH) (L)
	Novulin N (NPH) (NN)
	Insulatard NPH human (NN)

TABLE 9-4 Insulin (Continued)

Type	Product*
LONG-ACTING	
Onset 4–6 h	Ultralente (NN)
Peak 10–30 h	Iletin II PZI (L)
Duration 24–36 h	Iletin I PZI (L)
	Iletin I ultralente (L)
	Humulin U (ultralente) (L)
	Mixtard (NN)
	Humulin 70/30 (L)
	Novolin 70/30 (NN)
	Mixtard human 70/30 (NN)

* Note: All insulins listed are U-100.

† Manufacturers: L, Lilly; NN, NovoNordisk.

TABLE 9-5 Oral Hypoglycemic Agents

Agent	Duration of Action	How Given
First Generation Sulfonyureas		
Tolbutamide (Orinase)	6–10 h	Divided doses
Chorpropamide (Diabinese)	36–60 h	Single dose
Acetohexamide (Dymelor)	10–20 h	Single or divided doses
Tolazamide (Tolinase)	12–24 h	Single or divided doses
Second Generation Sulfonyureas		
Glyburide (Micronase, Diabeta, Glynase)	12–24 h	Single or divided doses
Glipizide (Glibenese, Glucatrol)	10–18 h	Single or divided doses
(Glucatrol XL)	24 h	Single daily dose
Biguanides		
Metformin (Glucophage)	12–24 h	Divided doses

TABLE 9-6 Signs and Symptoms of Diabetic Ketoacidosis (DKA)

••

Onset 1–24 h
Laboratory findings
  Blood glucose >250 mg/dL
  Ketonemia and presence of ketones in the urine
  Decreased plasma pH (<7.3) and bicarbonate (<15 mEq/L)
Dehydration caused by hyperglycemia
  Warm, dry skin
  Dry mucous membranes
  Tachycardia
  Weak, thready pulse
  Acute weight loss
  Hypotension
Ketoacidosis
  Anorexia, nausea, and vomiting
  Odor of ketones on the breath
  Depression of the central nervous system
    Lethargy and fatigue
    Stupor
    Coma
  Abdominal pain
Compensatory responses
  Rapid, deep respirations (Kussmaul's respiration)

••

TABLE 9-7 Signs and Symptoms of HHNS

••

Onset insidious: 24 h–2 wk
Laboratory findings
  Blood glucose >600 mg/dL
  Serum osmolarity ≥300 mOsm/L
Severe dehydration
  Dry skin and mucous membranes
  Extreme thirst
Neurologic manifestations
  Depressed sensorium, lethargy to coma
  Neurologic deficits
    Positive Babinski's sign
    Paresis or paralysis
    Sensory impairment
    Hyperthermia
    Hemianopia
Seizures

••

TABLE 9-8 Signs and Symptoms of Insulin Reaction

••

Onset sudden
Laboratory findings
   Blood glucose <50 mg/dL
Impaired cerebral function (caused by decreased glucose availability for brain
   metabolism)
   Feelings of vagueness
   Headache
   Difficulty in problem solving
   Slurred speech
   Impaired motor function
   Change in emotional behavior
   Seizures
   Coma
Autonomic nervous system responses
   Hunger
   Anxiety
   Hypotension
   Sweating
   Vasoconstriction of skin vessels (skin is pale and cool)
   Tachycardia

••

TABLE 9-9 Systematic Assessment of Arterial Blood Gases (ABG)

••

The following steps are recommended to evaluate arterial
blood gas values. They are based on the assumption that
the average values are

$$pH = 7.4$$
$$Pa_{CO_2} = 40 \text{ mm Hg}$$
$$H_{CO_3} = 24 \text{ mEq/L}$$

I. First, look at the pH. It can be high, low, or normal as
   follows:

$$pH > 7.4 \text{ (alkalosis)}$$
$$pH < 7.4 \text{ (acidosis)}$$
$$pH = 7.4 \text{ (normal)}$$

A normal pH may indicate perfectly normal blood gases,
or it may be an indication of a compensated imbalance.
A compensated imbalance is one in which the body has
been able to correct the pH by either respiratory or

(continued)

TABLE 9-9 Systematic Assessment of Arterial Blood Gases (ABG) (Continued)
••

metabolic changes (depending on the primary problem). For example, a patient with primary metabolic acidosis starts out with a low bicarbonate level but a normal carbon dioxide level. Soon afterward, the lungs try to compensate for the imbalance by exhaling large amounts of carbon dioxide (hyperventilation).

Another example: a patient with primary respiratory acidosis starts out with a high carbon dioxide level; soon afterward, the kidneys attempt to compensate by retaining bicarbonate. If the compensatory maneuver is able to restore the bicarbonate: carbonic acid ratio back to 20:1, full compensation (and thus normal pH) will be achieved.

II. The next step is to determine the primary cause of the disturbance. This is done by evaluating the $Paco_2$ and Hco_3 in relation to the pH.

1. pH > 7.4 (alkalosis)

If the $Paco_2$ is <40 mm Hg, the primary disturbance is respiratory alkalosis. (This situation occurs when a patient hyperventilates and "blows off" too much carbon dioxide. Recall that carbon dioxide dissolved in water becomes carbonic acid, the acid side of the "carbonic acid:base bicarbonate" buffer system.)

If the Hco_3 is >24 mEq/L, the primary disturbance is metabolic alkalosis. (This situation occurs when the body gains too much bicarbonate, an alkaline substance. Bicarbonate is the basic, or alkaline, side of the "carbonic acid:base bicarbonate" buffer system.)

2. pH < 7.4 (acidosis)

If the $Paco_2$ is >40 mm Hg, the primary disturbance is respiratory acidosis. (This situation occurs when a patient hypoventilates and thus retains too much carbon dioxide, an acidic substance.)

If the Hco_3 is <24 mEq/L, the primary disturbance is metabolic acidosis. (This situation occurs when the body's bicarbonate level drops, either because of direct bicarbonate loss or because of gains of acids such as lactic acid or ketones.)

III. The next step involves determining if compensation has begun.

This is done by lookizng at the value other than the primary disorder. If it is moving in the same direction as

TABLE 9-9 Systematic Assessment of Arterial Blood Gases (ABG) (Continued)

••

the primary value, compensation is under way. Consider the following gases:

Example:

	pH	$Paco_2$	Hco_3
(1)	7.20	60 mm Hg	24 mEq/L
(2)	7.40	60 mm Hg	37 mEq/L

The first set (1) indicates acute respiratory acidosis without compensation (the $Paco_2$ is high, the Hco_3 is normal). The second set (2) indicates chronic respiratory acidosis. Note that compensation has taken place; that is, the Hco_3 has elevated to an appropriate level to balance the high $Paco_2$ and produce a normal pH.

••

TABLE 9-10 Changes in Arterial Blood Gases in Metabolic Acid–Base Imbalances

••

Imbalance	pH	Hco_3	$Paco_2$	Base Excess
METABOLIC ACIDOSIS				
Uncompensated metabolic acidosis	↓	↓	N	↓
Partly compensated metabolic acidosis	↓	↓	↓	↓
Completely compensated metabolic acidosis	N	↓	↓	↓
METABOLIC ALKALOSIS				
Uncompensated (acute) metabolic alkalosis	↑	↑	N	↑
Partly compensated (subacute) metabolic alkalosis	↑	↑	↑	↑
Completely compensated (chronic) metabolic alkalosis	N	↑	↑	↑

••

N, normal.

TABLE 9-11 Compensatory Changes Related to Primary Acid–Base Disturbances

Imbalance	Primary Change	Compensatory Change
Metabolic acidosis (base bicarbonate deficit)	HCO_3 decreased	$1.5(HCO_3) + 8 \pm 2$
Metabolic alkalosis (base bicarbonate excess)	HCO_3 increased	0.6 mm Hg increase in $PaCO_2$ for every 1 mEq/L rise in HCO_3
Respiratory acidosis (carbonic acid excess)		
• Acute	$PaCO_2$ increased	1.0 mEq/L increase in HCO_3 for every 10 mm Hg rise in $PaCO_2$
• Chronic	$PaCO_2$ increased	3.5 mEq/L increase in HCO_3 for every 10 mm Hg rise in $PaCO_2$
Respiratory alkalosis (carbonic acid deficit)		
• Acute	$PaCO_2$ decreased	2.0 mEq/L decrease in HCO_3 for every 10 mm Hg fall in $PaCO_2$
• Chronic	$PaCO_2$ decreased	5.0 mEq/L decrease in HCO_3 for every 10 mm Hg fall in $PaCO_2$

TABLE 9-12 Fasting Blood Sugar (FBS)*

Age	mg/dL	*or*	nmol/L
0–7 d	30–100		1.7–5.6
7 d–6 y	74–127		4.2–7.0
6–18 y	70–106		3.9–6.0
Adult	65–110		3.5–6.1

* Normal values.

TABLE 9-13 Glycosylated Hemoglobin*

Results are expressed as percentage of total hemoglobin.

Normal (nondiabetic):	5.5%–8.5%
Diabetes:	Good control, 7.5%–11.4%
	Moderate control, 11.5%–15%
	Poor control, >15%

* Normal values.

TABLE 9-14 Glucose Tolerance Test*

FASTING

Adult:	70–110 mg/dL; 3.9–6.1 mmol/L
Child:	<130 mg/dL; <72 mmol/L

30 MINUTE

Adult:	110–170 mg/dL; 6.1–9.4 mmol/L

60 MINUTE (1 H)

Adult:	120–170 mg/dL; 6.7–9.4 mmol/L
Child:	<140 mg/dL

120 MINUTE (2 H)

Adult:	70–120 mg/dL; 3.9–6.7 mmol/L
Child:	<140 mg/dL; <7.8 mmol/L

3 HOUR

Adult:	70–120 mg/dL; 3.9–6.7 mmol/L

All four blood values must fall within normal limits to be considered normal. All urine samples also should test negative for glucose.

* Normal values.

CHAPTER 10

Hematologic and Immunologic Reference Facts

TABLE 10-1 Characteristics of White Blood Cells

Cell	Major Function	Physical Characteristics
Neutrophil	Ingest and destroy micro-organisms (phagocytosis)	Small cell, multilobed nucleus, most plentiful leukocyte
Eosinophil	Host resistance to helminthic infections; also allergic response	Bilobed nucleus; red-staining granules
Basophil	Allergic response	Bilobed nucleus; granules containing heparin and histamine
Monocyte	Phagocytosis	Large cell, kidney-shaped nucleus
B lymphocyte	Production of antibodies (immunoglobulins); humoral immunity	Small, agranular
T lymphocyte	Regulation of immune response; cellular immunity	Small, agranular; include cytotoxic, helper (T4), and suppressor (T8) T cells; identified by surface markers

TABLE 10-2 Blood Group Antigens and Antibodies

Blood Group	Antigen on RBC	Antibody in Plasma	Approximate Frequency of Occurrence in Population
A	A	Anti-B	45%
B	B	Anti-A	8%
AB	A and B	None	3%
O	None	Anti-A and anti-B	44%

TABLE 10-3 ABO and Rh Compatibility

Recipient	A	B	O	AB	Rh Positive	Rh Negative
WHOLE BLOOD						
A	●					
B		●				
O			●			
AB				●		
Rh positive					●	●
Rh negative						●
RED BLOOD CELLS						
A	●		●			
B		●	●			
O			●			
AB	●	●	●	●		
Rh positive					●	●
Rh negative						●
PLASMA						
A	●			●		
B		●		●		
O	●	●	●	●		
AB				●		
Rh positive					●	●
Rh negative					●	●

The chart above identifies ABO and Rh compatibility when transfusing whole blood, red blood cells, and plasma. Components suspended in plasma, such as platelets and cryoprecipitate, usually follow plasma compatibility rules if the total volume exceeds 102 mL for an adult patient.

TABLE 10-4 Acute Reactions to Blood Transfusion

Acute Reaction	Cause	Clinical Manifestations	Management	Prevention
Allergic	Sensitivity to plasma protein or donor antibody, which reacts with recipient antigen	Flushing Itching, rash Urticaria, hives Asthmatic wheezing Laryngeal edema Anaphylaxis	1. Stop transfusion immediately. Keep vein open (KVO) with normal saline. Notify health care provider and blood bank. 2. Give antihistamine as directed (diphenhydramine). 3. Observe for anaphylaxis—prepare epinephrine if respiratory distress is severe. 4. If hives are the only clinical manifestation, the transfusion can sometimes continue at a slower rate. 5. Send blood samples and blood bags to blood bank. Collect urine samples for testing.	Before transfusion, ask patient about past reactions. If patient has history of anaphylaxis, alert physician, have emergency drugs available, and remain at bedside for the first 30 min.
Febrile, nonhemolytic	Hypersensitivity to donor WBCs, platelets, or plasma proteins	Sudden chills and fever Headache Flushing Anxiety	1. Stop transfusion immediately and KVO with normal saline. Notify physician and blood bank.	Give antipyretic (acetaminophen or aspirin) before transfusion as directed.

(continued)

TABLE 10-4 Acute Reactions to Blood Transfusion (Continued)

Acute Reaction	Cause	Clinical Manifestations	Management	Prevention
Febrile, nonhemolytic (*cont.*)			2. Send blood samples and blood bags to blood bank. Collect urine samples for testing. 3. Check temperature ½ h after chill and as indicated thereafter. 4. Give antipyretics as prescribed—treat symptomatically.	Leukocyte-poor blood products may be recommended for future transfusions.
Septic reactions	Transfusion of blood or components contaminated with bacteria	Rapid onset of chills High fever Vomiting; diarrhea Marked hypotension	1. Stop transfusion immediately and KVO with normal saline. Notify physician and blood bank. 2. Obtain cultures of patient's blood and return blood bags with administration set to blood bank for culture. 3. Treat septicemia as directed—antibiotics, IV fluids, vasopressors, steroids.	Do not permit blood to stand at room temperature longer than necessary. Warm temperatures promote bacterial growth. Inspect blood for gas bubbles, clotting, or abnormal color before transfusion. Complete infusions within 4 h. Change administration set after 4 h of use.

Circulatory overload	Fluid administered at a rate or volume greater than the circulatory system can accommodate. Increased blood in pulmonary vessels and decreased lung compliance.	Rise in venous pressure Distended neck veins Dyspnea Cough Crackles at base of lungs	1. Stop transfusion and KVO with normal saline. Notify physician. 2. Place patient upright with feet in dependent position. 3. Administer prescribed diuretics, oxygen, morphine, and aminophylline.	Concentrated blood products should be given whenever possible. Transfuse at a rate within the circulatory reserve of the patient. Monitor central venous pressure of patient with heart disease.
Hemolytic reaction	Infusion of incompatible blood products: 1. Antibodies in recipient's plasma attach to transfused RBCs, hemolyzing the cells either in circulation or in the reticuloendothelial system.	Chills; fever Low back pain Feeling of head fullness; flushing Oppressive feeling Tachycardia, tachypnea Hypotension, vascular collapse Hemoglobinuria, hemoglobinemia	1. Stop transfusion immediately—KVO with 0.9% saline. 2. Notify physician and blood bank. 3. Treat shock, if present. 4. Draw testing samples, collect urine sample. 5. Maintain blood pressure with IV colloid solutions. Give diuretics as prescribed to maintain urine flow, glomerular filtration, and renal blood flow.	Meticulously verify patient identification—from sample collection to product infusion. Begin infusion slowly and observe closely for 30 min—consequences are in proportion to the amount of incompatible blood transfused.

(continued)

TABLE 10-4 Acute Reactions to Blood Transfusion (Continued)

Acute Reaction	Cause	Clinical Manifestations	Management	Prevention
Hemolytic reaction *(cont.)*	Infusion of incompatible blood products *(cont.)*: 2. Antibodies in donor plasma attach to recipient RBCs, causing hemolysis (may result from infusion of incompatible plasma—less severe than incompatible RBCs).	Bleeding Acute renal failure	6. Insert indwelling catheter to monitor hourly urine output. Patient may require dialysis if renal failure occurs.	

TABLE 10-5 Delayed Reactions to Transfusion Therapy

Delayed Reaction	Cause	Clinical Manifestations	Management	Prevention
Delayed hemolytic reaction	The destruction of transfused RBCs by antibody not detectable during crossmatch, but formed rapidly after transfusion. Rapid production may occur because of antigen exposure during previous transfusions or pregnancy.	Fever Mild jaundice Decreased hematocrit	Generally, no acute treatment is required, but hemolysis may be severe enough to cause shock and renal failure. If this occurs, manage as outlined under acute hemolytic reactions (Table 10-4).	The crossmatch blood sample should be drawn within 3 d of blood transfusion. Antibody formation may occur within 90 d of transfusion and/or pregnancy.
Iron overload (hemosiderosis)	Deposition of iron in the heart, endocrine organs, liver, spleen, skin, and other major organs as a result of multiple, long-term transfusions (as in aplastic anemia, thalassemia).	Diabetes Decreased thyroid function Arrhythmias CHF and other symptoms related to major organ failure	1. Treat symptomatically. 2. Deferoxamine (Desferal), which chelates, and removes accumulated iron through the kidneys; administered IV, IM, or SC.	

(continued)

TABLE 10-5 Delayed Reactions to Transfusion Therapy (Continued)

Delayed Reaction	Cause	Clinical Manifestations	Management	Prevention
Graft-versus-host disease	Engraftment of lymphocytes in the bone marrow of immunosuppressed patients, setting up an immune response of the graft against the host	Erythematous skin rash Liver function test abnormalities Profuse, watery diarrhea	1. Immunosuppression with corticosteroids, cyclosporine A 2. Symptomatic management of pruritus, pain 3. Fluid and electrolyte replacement for diarrhea	Transfuse with irradiated blood products.
Infectious disease Hepatitis B	Hepatitis B virus transmitted from blood donor to recipient via infected blood products	Elevated liver enzymes (SGPT and SGOT) Anorexia, malaise Nausea and vomiting Fever Dark urine Jaundice	Usually resolves spontaneously within 4–6 wk. Can result in permanent liver damage. Treat symptomatically.	Screen blood donors, temporarily rejecting those who may have had contact with the virus. Those with a history of hepatitis after age 11 are permanently deferred; pretest all blood products (EIA).
Hepatitis C (formerly non-A, non-B hepatitis)	Hepatitis C virus transmitted from blood donor to recipient via infected blood products	Similar to serum B hepatitis, but symptoms are usually less severe. Chronic	Symptoms usually mild and require no treatment.	Pretest all blood donors (ALT, anti-HBc antibody, anti–hepatitis C antibody).

		liver disease and cirrhosis may develop.		Question prospective blood donors regarding colds, flu, foreign travel.
Epstein-Barr virus, cytomegalovirus, malaria	Transmitted through infected blood products			Test each donor for HIV antibody.
Acquired immunodeficiency syndrome	HIV virus transmitted from blood donor to recipient via infected blood products	Night sweats Unexplained weight loss Lymphadenopathy Pneumocystis pneumonia Kaposi's sarcoma Diarrhea	AZT may delay onset of AIDS symptoms. Active disease is treated symptomatically.	Reject prospective high-risk donors: males who have had sex with another male since 1977; users of self-injected IV drugs; male or female partners of prostitutes; hemophiliacs or their sexual partners; sexual partners of those with AIDS or high risk for AIDS; immigrants from Haiti or sub-Saharan Africa.

(continued)

TABLE 10-5 Delayed Reactions to Transfusion Therapy (Continued)

Delayed Reaction	Cause	Clinical Manifestations	Management	Prevention
HTLV-1–associated myelopathy and tropical spastic paraparesis (HAM/TSP) Adult T-cell leukemia	Human T-lymphotropic virus type 1 (HTLV-1) transmitted from blood donor to recipient via blood products.	Signs of neuromuscular disease Signs of T-cell leukemia	HTLV-1–infected individuals have a low risk of developing disease (3–5%). Incubation period 10–20 y. Should disease occur, treat symptomatically	Screen all prospective blood donors for anti–HTLV-1 antibody.
Syphilis	Spirochetemia caused by *Treponema pallidum.* Incubation 4–18 wk	Presence of chancre Regional lymphadenopathy Generalized rash	Penicillin therapy	Test blood before transfusion (rapid plasma reagin—RPR). Organism does not remain viable in blood stored 24–48 h at 4°C.

TABLE 10-6 Guide for Adult Immunization

Age (y)	Vaccine	Comments
18–24	Td* (0.5 mL IM)	Booster every 10 y at mid-decade (eg, age 25, 35, 45) for those who completed primary series
	Measles† (MMR, 0.5 mL SC × 1 or 2)	Post–high school institutions should require two doses of live measles vaccine (separated by 1 mo), the first dose preferably given before entry
	Mumps‡ (MMR, 0.5 mL SC × 1)	Especially susceptible males
	Rubella‡ (MMR, 0.5 mL SC × 1)	Especially susceptible females; pregnancy now or within 3 mo postvaccination is contraindication to vaccination
	Influenza	Advocated for young adults at increased risk of exposure (eg, military recruits, students in dorms)
25–64	Td*	As above
	Mumps‡	As above
	Measles† (MMR, 0.5 mL SC × 1)	Persons vaccinated between 1963 and 1967 may have received inactivated vaccine and should be revaccinated
	Rubella‡ (MMR, 0.5 mL SC × 1)	Principally females ≤45 y with childbearing potential; pregnancy now or within 3 mo postvaccination is contraindication to vaccination

(continued)

TABLE 10-6 Guide for Adult Immunization (Continued)

Age (y)	Vaccine	Comments
>65	Td*	As above
	Influenza (0.5 mL IM)	Annually, usually in November
	Pneumococcal (23 valent, 0.5 mL IM)	Single dose; efficacy for elderly not established, but case control and epidemiology studies suggest 60–70% effectiveness in preventing pneumococcal bacteremia (*NEJM* 325:1453, 1991)

IM: intramuscular; MMR: measles, mumps, and rubella; SC: subcutaneously.

* Td—Diphtheria and tetanus toxoids absorbed (for adult use). Primary series is 0.5 mL IM at 0, 4 wk, and 6–12 mo; booster doses at 10-year intervals are single doses of 0.5 mL IM. Adults who have not received at least 3 doses of Td should complete the primary series. Persons with unknown histories should receive the series.

† Persons are considered immune to measles if there is documentation of receipt of two doses of live measles vaccine after the first birthday, prior physician diagnosis of measles, laboratory evidence of measles immunity, or birth before 1957.

‡ Persons are considered immune to mumps if they have a record of adequate vaccination, documented physician-diagnosed disease, or laboratory evidence of immunity. Persons are considered immune to rubella if they have a record of vaccination after their first birthday or laboratory evidence of immunity. (A physician diagnosis of rubella is considered nonspecific.)

From: Bartlett, John G. Pocket Book of Infectious Disease Therapy. Baltimore: Williams & Wilkins, 1993.

(Adapted from American College of Physicians. Guide for Adult Immunization, 2nd ed. Philadelphia: American College of Physicians, 1990; MMWR 40(RR12):1–94, 1991.)

TABLE 10-7 Opportunistic Infections and Drug Therapies

Name	Clinical Manifestations	Diagnostic Tests	Medications
Pneumocystis carinii pneumonia (PCP)	Cough; dry or scant white sputum production Shortness of breath Low grade fever	Chest x-ray Sputum culture for silver stain Bronchoscopy	Trimethoprim/ sulfamethoxazole (Bactrim) Pentamidine (Pentam) (IV only) Dapsone (Dapsone)
Candida esophagitis/oral	White coating in mouth White coating down throat Sensation of food getting caught in throat while swallowing	Gross observation Microscopy for hyphae Endoscopy	Nystatin (Mycostatin) Clotrimazole (Mycelex) Ketoconazole (Nizoral) Fluconazole (Diflucan) Amphotericin B (Fungizone)
Mycobacterium avium complex (MAC)	Weakness Weight loss Diarrhea Fever, chills	Blood culture for acid-fast bacteria	Micobutin (Rifabutin) Rifampin (Rifadin) Ethambutol (Myambutol) Isoniazid (INH) Clarithromycin (Biaxin)
Kaposi's sarcoma	Pink, purple, or brown spots Pain, edema of affected area	Gross observation Biopsy	Alpha-interferon (Alferon) Vincristine (Oncovin) Bleomycin (Blenoxane)

(continued)

TABLE 10-7 Opportunistic Infections and Drug Therapies (Continued)

Name	Clinical Manifestations	Diagnostic Tests	Medications
Toxoplasmosis	Fever Headache Change in mental status Confusion Lethargy Frank psychosis	Computed tomography Magnetic resonance imaging Serum *Toxoplasma* antibodies	Pyrimethamine (Daraprim) Sulfadiazine (Microsulfon) Clindamycin (Cleocin)
Tuberculosis	Cough; dry or scant frothy white/pink sputum Shortness of breath Fever Lymphadenopathy	Positive purified protein derivative (≥5 mm induration) Chest x-ray Sputum culture for acid-fast bacteria	Isoniazid (INH) Rifampin (Rifadin) Pyrazinamide (Daraprim) Ethambutol (Myambutol)
Cryptosporidium	Severe diarrhea Severe abdominal cramping	Stool culture for *Cryptosporidium*	Octreotide (Somatostatin)
Cryptococcal meningitis	Headache Confusion, memory loss Nausea Seizures Change in mental status Fever Photophobia	Cerebral spinal fluid culture for cryp- tococcosis	Amphotericin B (Fungizone) Flucytosine (Ancobon) Fluconazole (Diflucan)

Condition	Signs/Symptoms	Diagnostic Tests	Treatment
Cytomegalovirus (CMV)	Visual changes; floaters/blindness Difficulty swallowing Nausea, vomiting Abdominal cramping	Ophthalmologic examination Blood, urine, tissue culture for CMV	Gancyclovir (Cytorene) Foscarnet (Foscavir)

HIV encephalopathy/AIDS dementia complex	Early
	  Inattention
	  Reduced concentration
	  Forgetfulness
	  Slowed movements
	  Clumsiness
	  Ataxia
	  Apathy
	  Agitation
	Late
	  Paraplegia
	  Mutism
	  Vegetative state
		Computed tomography
		Magnetic resonance imaging
		Cerebral spinal fluid evaluation
			Zidovudine (Retrovir, AZT)—high doses

TABLE 10-8 Characteristics and Management of Genital Lesions Caused by STDs

Disorder and Incubation	Clinical Manifestations	Diagnostic and Treatment
Herpes genitalis—5–20 d	Clustered vesicles on erythematous, edematous base that rupture leaving shallow, painful ulcer that eventually crusts; mild regional lymphadenopathy; recurrent and may be brought on by stress, infection, pregnancy, sunburn	Diagnostic tests include Tzanck smear, viral culture, or antigen test of tissue or exudate from lesion. No cure, but symptomatic period is diminished by acyclovir (Zovirax) started with each recurrence; or recurrences greatly reduced or prevented by continuous treatment. Analgesics and sitz baths promote comfort.
Syphilis—10–90 d for primary; up to 6 mo following lesion (chancre) for secondary	Primary: nontender, shallow, indurated, clean ulcer; mild regional lymphadenopathy Secondary: maculopapular rash including palms and soles, mucous patches, and condylomatous lesions; fever, generalized lymphadenopathy	VDRL or rapid plasma reagin (RPR) blood test with confirmation by specific treponemal antibody tests Preferred treatment is benzathine penicillin G (Bicillin LA) 2.4 million units IM in a single dose; doxycycline (Vibramycin), tetracycline (Tetracyn), and possibly erythromycin (Eryc) may be used.
Chancroid—2–10 d	Vesiculopustule that erodes, leaving a tender, shallow or deep, well circumscribed ulcer with ragged, or deep, well circumscribed ulcer with ragged	May be identified on Gram, Giemsa, or Wright stain; must be cultured on special media

	undermined borders and a friable base covered by purulent exudate; unilateral or bilateral large, tender inguinal lymph nodes (buboes) in 50% of patients.	Treated with azithromycin (Zithromax), erythromycin (Eryc), or ceftriaxone (Rocephin) IM; single dose regimens are available. Apply warm soaks to buboes.
LGV—3–21 d	Small, transient, nontender papule or superficial ulcer precedes firm, adherent unilateral inguinal and femoral lymph nodes (buboes) with characteristic groove in between (groove sign); may suppurate	Microimmunofluorescence testing of bubo aspirate Treatment of choice is doxycycline (Vibramycin), but erythromycin (Eryc) may be effective. Incision and excision of buboes should be avoided; aspiration may be helpful.
Condyloma acuminatum—3 wk to 3 mo, possibly years before grossly visible	Single or multiple, soft, fleshy, flat or vegetating growth(s) may occur on penis, anal area, urethra; no lymphadenopathy	Diagnosed by Pap smear or biopsy Topical therapy with podofilox 0.5% (Condylox) for external warts, podophyllin 10–25% solution, or trichloroacetic acid 80–90% (TCA)—may require multiple applications. Cryotherapy, electrodissection, electrocautery, carbon dioxide laser, and surgical excision may also be done. Recurrence is common.

TABLE 10-9 Sexually Transmitted Diseases and Laboratory Diagnoses

Disease*	Causative Agents†	Diagnosis
Chancroid	*Haemophilus*	Culture of lesion or aspirate. Differential diagnosis should include syphilis, herpes, and LAV monoclonal antibody test, DNA probes.
Gonorrhea	*Neisseria gonorrhoeae*	Gram stain of male urethra, culture of male urethra or female cervix, rectum, or pharynx. When indicated, urogenital swab tested for direct antigen.
Granuloma inguinale (donovanosis)	*Calymmatobacterium granulomatis* (formerly *Donovania granulomatis*)	Wright's Giemsa stain of lesion, tissue biopsy.
Hepatitis B	Hepatitis B virus (HBV)	Serologic testing HB, AG—most infectious state of disease. HB, AG: presence and persistence of infectivity and chronicity usually appear before symptoms.
Genital herpes	Herpes simplex virus (HSV) types 1 and 2	Culture from unroofed blister, scrapings examined by fluorescent microscopy or cytologic stains
Lymphogranuloma venereum (LGV)	*Chlamydia trachomatis* serotypes L_1, L_2, and L_3	Culture of aspirate of bubo, serologic tests of blood (immunofluorescence and enzyme immunoassay).
Molluscum contagiosum	Molluscum contagiosum virus	Clinical appearance of lesions (pearly white, painless, umbilicated papules), microscopic exam of scrapings.
Chlamydia	*Chlamydia trachomatis* serotypes D–K	Cell culture, urogenital swabs for direct antigen test, or fluorescent microscopy.
Candidosis (monilia)	*Candida albicans*	Culture, KOH wet mount, Gram stain.

Pelvic inflammatory disease (PID)	*Neisseria gonorrhoeae*, *Chlamydia trachomatis*	Clinical symptoms, cervical culture, laparoscopy or culdocentesis.
Pediculosis pubis	*Phthirus pubis* (pubic or crab louse)	Adult lice or nits appear on body hairs.
Scabies	*Sarcoptes scabiei*	Characteristic lesions, scrapings for microscopy.
Syphilis	*Treponema pallidum*	Darkfield microscopic examination of primary and secondary lesions for *T. pallidum*. Nontreponemal reagin tests (VDRL, RPR) and specific tests (FTA-ABS, MHA-TP) are used to identify active and latent syphilis.
Trichomoniasis	*Trichomonas vaginalis*	Vaginal, urethral, prostatic secretion examined microscopically in a drop of saline for motile trichomonas; culture; speculum exam reveals foamy, greenish discharge and presence of bright red dots in vaginal wall and cervix.
Nonspecific urethritis (nongonococcal urethritis—NGU)	*Chlamydia trachomatis* (50% of cases), *Ureaplasma urealyticum*, a human T-strain mycoplasma (*Mycoplasma hominis*), *Trichomonas vaginalis*, *Candida albicans*, herpes simplex virus	Failure to demonstrate *N. gonorrheae* in cell culture; culture of genital specimen, tissue, urine.

(continued)

TABLE 10-9 Sexually Transmitted Diseases and Laboratory Diagnoses (Continued)

Disease*	Causative Agents†	Diagnosis
Nonspecific vaginitis	*Gardnerella vaginalis* *Mobiluncus cortisii* *M. mulieris*	Wet mount for "clue" cells or PAP smear; fishy smell is released when specimen fluid is mixed with 10% KOH. Culture or enzyme immunoassay to RD gonorrhea.
Condylomata acuminata (venereal warts)	Human papilloma DNA virus	Typical clinical lesion; cauliflower-like, soft, pink growths around vulva, anus, labia, vagina, glans penis, urethra and perineum; rule out syphilis.
Acquired immunodeficiency syndrome (AIDS)	HIV virus	Serology
Gastrointestinal amebiasis (giardiasis), shigellosis, campylobacteriosis, and anorectal infections	Enteric infections: *Giardia lamblia, Entamoeba histolytica, Cryptosporidium* spp. *Shigella* spp., *Campylobacter fetus,* *Strongyloides* spp. (worms)	Stool–polyvinyl alcohol fixative or formalin ethyl acetate sedimentation (FES); same as above. Stool stain Rectal stool swab culture Rectal stool swab culture Stool (FES)

Anorectal:

Neisseria gonorrhoeae	Anal canal swab specimen, culture
Chlamydia trachomatis	Anal swab or rectal biopsy culture
Treponema pallidum	Dark-field microscopy plus serology, lesion swab, culture
Herpes simplex virus	Signs and symptoms, tissue culture
Human papillomavirus	Signs and symptoms, tissue culture

* The major diseases are syphilis and gonorrhea.

† The pathogens causing sexually transmitted diseases span the full range of medical microbiology. The only common characteristic of these pathogens is that they may cause genital disease or may be transmitted by genital contact.

TABLE 10-10 Selected Infectious Diseases

Disease and Infectious Agent	Clinical Manifestations	Incubation Period	Diagnostic Tests
VECTOR-TRANSMITTED FEVERS			
Rocky Mountain spotted fever *Rickettsia rickettsii*	Systemic, febrile illness Rash usually occurs by the 6th day with a progression from macular to maculopapular to petechial. Fever, headache, myalgia, nausea, and vomiting	Related to the size of the inoculum Usually 1 wk, with a range of 1–14 d	Immunofluorescence of body tissue may identify rickettsiae during the 3rd or 4th day of illness. Serology—increase in antibody titer can usually be detected after 7–10 d of illness, but may be delayed for 4 or more weeks if antibiotic therapy is begun early. Titers wane rapidly in late convalescence. Complement fixation—titers rise later in illness (10–14th day) and persist longer.
Lyme disease *Borrelia burgdorferi*	Erythema migrans is the best clinical marker— an annular skin lesion that appears at the site of the tick bite and expands over a period of days to weeks and develops central clearing. Lesion is warm to touch but not painful.	3–32 d	IgM antibodies peak during the 3rd to 6th weeks after disease onset. IgG antibodies slowly rise and peak months later when arthritis is present. Early in the illness, high sedimentation rate, elevated serum IgM level, or an

Management	Complications	Nursing Considerations
Tetracycline (Sumycin) (25–50 mg/kg/d) or chloramphenicol (Chloromycetin) (50 mg/kg/d) administered orally in 4 divided doses. Appropriate doses of IV preparations may be substituted during the initial toxic state. Medication continued for 5–7 d. Supportive therapy including fluid replacement, control of fever, and management of anemia with transfusion of packed red cells.	Shock Disseminated intravascular coagulation (DIC) Thrombosis and gangrene Cardiac arrhythmias Neurologic sequelae Renal failure Coma and death	1. Not communicable person to person. 2. Instruct the patient that relapse of illness may occur and that recurrence of symptoms should be reported immediately. 3. The best means of prevention is the avoidance of tick-infested areas. While working or playing in infested areas, inspection of the body and clothing should be performed every 3–4 h. 4. Ticks should be removed from the skin with tweezers or forceps to avoid leaving mouth parts in the skin. 5. Insect repellents are useful for repelling ticks.
Tetracycline (Sumycin) 250 mg qid or phenoxymethyl penicillin (Betapen-VK) 500 mg qid or erythromycin (Eryc) 250 mg qid for at least 10 days or up to 20 days if symptoms persist. For meningitis/cranial or peripheral neuropathies—IV penicillin G (Duracillin) 20 million units a day or ceftriaxone (Rocephin) 2 g/d	Meningeal irritation leading to meningitis, encephalitis Chorea Atrioventricular block	1. Not communicable person to person. 2. The best means of prevention is the avoidance of tick-infested areas. While working or playing in infested areas, inspection of the body and clothing should be performed every 3–4 h. 3. Ticks should be removed from the skin with tweezers or forceps to avoid leaving mouth

(continued)

TABLE 10-10 Selected Infectious Diseases
(Continued)
••

Disease and Infectious Agent	Clinical Manifestations	Incubation Period	Diagnostic Tests
Lyme disease *Borrelia burgdorferi* *(cont.)*	Flulike symptoms— malaise, fever, headache, stiff neck, myalgia Inflamed painful arthritis Limb weakness Bell's palsy		increased SGOT level
VIRAL INFECTIONS			
Influenza Types A, B, and C with many mutagenic strains	Acute, usually self-limited febrile illness associated with upper and lower respiratory infection Characterized by a severe and protracted cough, myalgias, coryza, and mild sore throat	24–72 h	Tissue culture of nasal or pharyngeal secretions Fluorescent antibody staining of secretions
Mononucleosis Epstein-Barr virus (EBV)	Produces a generalized lymph node hyperplasia Characterized by fever, exudative pharyngitis, splenomegaly, and	4–6 w	Differential WBC— lymphocytes and monocytes >50%, with more than 10% being atypical lymphocytes. Serology— heterophil

Management	Complications	Nursing Considerations
for 14–21 days. Lyme arthritis—IV penicillin G 20 million units a day for 10 days.		parts in the skin. 4. Insect repellents are useful for repelling ticks.
Aspirin (A.S.A.) or aceta-minophen (Tylenol) for control of fever. Amantadine (Symmetrel) 100 mg PO bid for duration of epidemic (5–6 wk) as prophy-laxis for high-risk persons. Amantadine is given as therapy within 24–48 h of symptoms until 48 h after symptoms resolve. Agent-specific antibiotics for bacterial complica-tions Vaccine must be repeated yearly in the fall for viral strain expected. Recommended for any person at risk for com-plications of influenza.	Secondary bacterial pneu-monia Primary viral pneumonia	1. Maintain bed rest for at least 48 h after fever subsides. 2. Force fluids. 3. Encourage high-risk persons to receive the influenza vaccine in the fall of each year. 4. Continue antibiotics prescribed for bacterial complications for defined time period (usually 7–10 d). 5. Report symptoms of secondary infection (purulent nasal drainage or sputum, ear pain, increase in fever) to health care provider.
Supportive therapy to in-clude aspirin (A.S.A.) or acetaminophen (Tylenol) for sore throat and fever, bed rest. Surgical removal of the spleen for splenic rupture.	Splenic rupture Thrombocytopenic purpura Hemolytic anemia Pericarditis Hepatitis Encephalitis	1. Convalescence may be as long as 3–4 wk. 2. Patients with splenomegaly should avoid activity that may increase the risk of in-jury to the spleen, such as contact sports and heavy lifting.

(continued)

TABLE 10-10 Selected Infectious Diseases
(Continued)

Disease and Infectious Agent	Clinical Manifestations	Incubation Period	Diagnostic Tests
Mononucleosis Epstein-Barr virus (EBV) *(cont.)*	lymphadenopathy		agglutination antibody present usually by the end of 1st week. Not useful diagnostic tool in children under 5 years of age. If negative, EBV IgM and IgG may be performed. EBV IgM elevated 1:80 to 1:160 drops rapidly after clinical disease. EBV IgG elevated 1:80 is suggestive, >1:5 suggests immunity.
Cytomegalovirus (CMV)	Ordinarily asymptomatic Clinical disease in the adult resembles mononucleosis. More extensive organ involvement in the immunosuppressed host—hepatitis, pneumonitis, arthralgias may occur. Congenital infections are serious and lead to irreversible CNS damage.	Unknown; 3–8 wk following transfusion; in neonates 3–12 wk following delivery-produced infection.	Differential WBC count—increase in lymphocytes, many atypical Complement fixation—fourfold rise in titer in adult or child suggestive of current infection Positive cell culture of urine, cervical secretions, or biopsy tissue Differential diagnosis: heterophil agglutination negative

Management	Complications	Nursing Considerations
Corticosteroids for severe neurologic complications, thrombocytopenic purpura, or hemolytic anemia.		3. Report any excess bruising or bleeding, jaundice, or abnormal CNS functioning.
Supportive therapy for control of fever and sore throat. Corticosteroids for neurologic and hematologic complications. Hyperimmune gamma globulin (Gammar) as a prophylactic agent for patients undergoing marrow transplantation.	Congenital infection leads to neurologic defects (severe mental retardation, microcephaly, psychomotor retardation). Immunocompromised host—progressive pneumonitis, hemolytic anemia, hepatitis, pericarditis, and GI ulceration.	1. Convalescence may be as long as 3–4 wk. 2. Patients with splenomegaly should avoid activity that may increase the risk of injury to the spleen, such as contact sports and heavy lifting. 3. Report any excess bruising or bleeding, jaundice, or abnormal CNS functioning.

(continued)

TABLE 10-10 Selected Infectious Diseases
(Continued)

. . . .

Disease and Infectious Agent	Clinical Manifestations	Incubation Period	Diagnostic Tests
Rabies Rabies virus	Initial symptoms nonspecific and consist of malaise, fatigue, headache, anorexia, and fever. May have pain or paresthesia at the site of exposure. Usually lasts 2–10 d. Followed by the acute neurologic period, which includes hyperactivity, disorientation, hallucinations, seizures, nuchal stiffness, or paralysis. In 50% or more of cases, hydrophobia (fear of water) is present. Usually lasts 2–7 d and ends with either death or onset of coma. Coma occurs 4–10 d after onset of symptoms and may last for hours or months. Respiratory arrest usually occurs, followed by death.	20–90 d Shorter when the site of the bite is on the head (25–48 d) than when it is on an extremity (46–78 d)	Measurement of rabies neutralizing antibody by the rapid fluorescent focus inhibition test Virus isolation from saliva, CSF, urine sediment, and tracheal secretions most successful in the first 2 weeks of clinical illness

Management	Complications	Nursing Considerations
Rabies is a disease best controlled through prevention rather than treatment.	Most complications occur in the coma phase and include:	1. No tests available to diagnose rabies before onset of clinical disease
Supportive therapy to manage neurologic, respiratory, and cardiac symptoms	Increases in intracranial pressure	2. Preexposure prophylaxis should be offered to persons at high risk for exposure to rabies, such as veterinarians, veterinary students, and certain laboratory workers with human diploid cell rabies vaccine (HDCV).
Isolation of the patient using masks, gowns, and gloves	Hypothalamic involvement producing inappropriate secretion of ADH (antidiuretic hormone) and/or diabetes insipidus	
Use of high-dose passive rabies immunoglobulin (Imogam) or vaccine (Imovax) after the onset of illness has not been successful.	Autonomic dysfunction leading to hypertension, hypotension, cardiac dysrhythmias or hypothermia	3. Bites from animals, particularly dogs and cats, should be thoroughly cleaned with soap and water immediately.
Interferon of unproven value	Hypoxia	4. Domestic dogs and cats should be quarantined for 10 d.
		5. Wild animal carriers include skunk, bat, fox, coyote, raccoon, bobcat, and other carnivores.
		6. Postexposure prophylaxis must include the use of human rabies immunoglobulin followed by HDCV unless preexposure prophylaxis with HDCV had been administered. HDCV requires 5 doses IM.

(continued)

TABLE 10-10 Selected Infectious Diseases
(Continued)

● ●

Disease and Infectious Agent	Clinical Manifestations	Incubation Period	Diagnostic Tests
PROTOZOAN INFECTIONS			
Malaria *Plasmodium vivax,* *P. falciparum,* *P. malariae,* and *P. ovale*	Malarial paroxysm characterized by high fever, chills, rigor is the hallmark of acute malaria. Prodromal period from 1 to several days before the onset of the paroxysms and may complain of malaise, headache, myalgia, and fatigue. Moderate splenomegaly and tender hepatomegaly. Coagulopathic.	Variable depending on the strain	Diagnosis of malaria rests on the demonstration of parasites in stained peripheral blood smears. Twice-daily smears on several days required. If more than 5% of the RBCs are parasitized, *P. falciparum* should also be suspected. Leukopenia, hemolytic anemia (normocytic, normochromic), platelets decreased ($<50,000/mm^3$). Urine reveals small amounts of protein. Liver function tests reveal elevated transaminase level and increase in indirect serum bilirubin.
Amebiasis *Entamoeba histolytica*	*Nondysenteric colitis:* Recurring episodes of loose stools. Vague abdominal pain. Hemorrhoids with	Variable—3 d to months; usually 2–4 wk	Microscopic examination of stool, rectal secretions; positive for trophozoites or cysts of protozoan.

Management	Complications	Nursing Considerations
Patients with *P. falciparum* infection should be hospitalized. If *P. falciparum* infection is ruled out, therapy with chloroquine (Aralen) can be instituted on an outpatient basis. General management should include: IV fluids and electrolytes—restrict fluids in cerebral edema. Assisted ventilation with pulmonary edema Dialysis in renal failure Transfusions in anemia Heparin or fresh-frozen plasma in coagulopathy	Splenic rupture Renal failure Hepatic failure Pulmonary edema Perivascular edema and hemorrhage in cerebral cortex Disseminated intravascular coagulation (DIC)	1. Patients with *P. vivax* or *P. ovale* may have recurrence of symptoms and should report them immediately. 2. Patients should return for blood examination 4–5 d after completion of treatment. 3. Travelers to malaria-endemic countries should follow preventive measures: Proper use of mosquito netting at night Clothing that minimizes contact with mosquitoes Use of insect repellents Chemoprophylaxis with chloroquine or hydroxychloroquine (Plaquenil).
Treatment regimens depend on the severity of the illness. Acute dysentery is best treated with metronidazole (Flagyl) followed by iodoquinol	Perforated bowel Hemorrhage Systemic deterioration Anemia Hepatic abscess	1. Instruct patient to wash hands thoroughly after defecating to prevent transmission to others. 2. Household and sexual contacts should seek medical examination

(continued)

TABLE 10-10 Selected Infectious Diseases
(Continued)

....

Disease and Infectious Agent	Clinical Manifestations	Incubation Period	Diagnostic Tests
Amebiasis *Entamoeba histolytica* *(cont.)*	occasional rectal bleeding. *Dysenteric colitis:* Intense, intermittent, bloody, mucous diarrhea.		
Giardiasis *Giardia lamblia*	*Acute:* Explosive, foul-smelling diarrheal stool Abdominal cramping and flatulence Nausea *Chronic:* Intermittent loose stools Increased flatulence and distention Vague abdominal discomfort	5–25 d; median 7–10 d	Examination of stool; positive for cysts or trophozoites of the *G. lamblia* protozoan

• •

Management	Complications	Nursing Considerations
(Diodoquin) if cyst passage persists.		and treatment. 3. Instruct patient on safe sexual practices. 4. Travelers to areas where the water supply is not chemically treated or protected from sewage should boil all water used for drinking and cooking. 5. Relapses after treatment are common. Follow-up should be scheduled at 6 wk and 6 mo after treatment.
Metronidazole (Flagyl) is the drug of choice. Quinacrine (Atabrine) is an alternative.	Chronic diarrhea Malabsorption	1. Instruct patient to wash hands thoroughly after defecating to prevent transmission to others. 2. Household and sexual contacts should seek medical examination and treatment. 3. Instruct patient on safe sexual practices. 4. Travelers to areas where the water supply is not chemically treated or protected from sewage should boil all water used for drinking and cooking. 5. Relapses after treatment are common. Follow-up should be scheduled at 6 wk and 6 mo after treatment.

(continued)

TABLE 10-10 **Selected Infectious Diseases**
(Continued)

••

Disease and Infectious Agent	Clinical Manifestations	Incubation Period	Diagnostic Tests
Hookworm *Ancylostoma duodenale, A. ceylonicum, Necator americanus*	Chronic debilitating disease leading to iron-deficiency anemia and hypoproteinemia that result from intestinal blood loss to the hookworm	Symptoms may develop after a few weeks to many months, depending on intensity of infection.	Microscopic examination of cultured specimen positive for larva
Trichinosis *Trichinella spiralis*	Clinical disease highly variable; can range from inapparent infection to a fulminating fatal disease Sudden appearance of muscle soreness and pain accompanied by edema of upper eyelids. Ocular signs progress to subconjunctival, subungual, and retinal hemorrhages; pain; photophobia Remittent fever is usual, sometimes as high as 104°F. Gastrointestinal symptoms such as diarrhea	5–45 d depending on the number of worms involved; usually 8–15 d after ingestion of infected meat	Skeletal muscle biopsy not earlier than 10 d after exposure to infection demonstrates the *Trichinella* larvae. Serology; complement fixation, fluorescent antibody—fourfold increase in antibody titer 2 wk after infection. Differential WBC count—increase in eosinophils

Management	Complications	Nursing Considerations
Mebendazole (Vermox) 100 mg bid for 3 d or pyrantel pamoate (Antiminth) single oral dose of 11 mg/kg up to total of 1 g/d. Iron therapy to correct anemia	Immunosuppressed individuals—septicemia and death	1. Follow-up examination of the stool 2 wk after therapy is necessary. 2. Nutrition counseling and taking iron supplements are recommended until deficiencies are corrected. 3. Family members and close contacts should be examined and treated for parasites. 4. Thorough hand washing after defecation is critical.
Thiabendazole (Mintezol) within 24 h of eating infected meat— 25 mg/kg/day for 1 wk Supportive therapy for respiratory, neurologic, and cardiac sequelae	Respiratory failure or pneumonia Myocarditis Encephalitis Death	1. Instruct patient to wash hands thoroughly after defecation. 2. Proper cooking of pork to 150°F is necessary. 3. Family members and close contacts of patients should be examined and treated for parasites.

(continued)

TABLE 10-10 Selected Infectious Diseases
(Continued)

••

Disease and Infectious Agent	Clinical Manifestations	Incubation Period	Diagnostic Tests
FUNGAL INFECTIONS			
Histoplasmosis *Histoplasma capsulatum*	May be asymptomatic with only hypersensitivity to histoplasmin Four other clinical forms of disease: 1. Acute pulmonary histoplasmosis characterized by pleural and substernal chest pain, fever, weakness, dry or productive cough, erythema multiforme, and erythema nodosum 2. Acute disseminated with hepatosplenomegaly, high fever, and prostration 3. Chronic pulmonary histoplasmosis characterized by purulent sputum, hemoptysis, and chronic low-grade fever	5–18 d after exposure, commonly 10 d	Complement fixation shows increase in antibodies within 3–4 wk; fourfold increase suggests disease progression. Fungal culture positive for *H. capsulatum* Chest x-ray—*Acute findings:* transient parenchymal pulmonary infiltrates resembling lobar pneumonia. *Chronic:* Progressively enlarging areas of necrosis with or without cavitation.

Management	Complications	Nursing Considerations
Amphotericin B (Fungi-zone) 5–10 mg initial dose, increasing 10 mg/d until 50 mg is attained, then 50 mg 3 times/wk until 2.5 g has been administered Corticosteroids and diphenhydramine (Benadryl) to mini-mize the side effects of amphotericin	Pneumonia Progressive emphysema Hepatosplenomegaly Severe prostration Death	1. Medical follow-up is indicated for 1 y after treatment to prevent relapses.

(continued)

TABLE 10-10 Selected Infectious Diseases
(Continued)

••

Disease and Infectious Agent	Clinical Manifestations	Incubation Period	Diagnostic Tests
Histoplasmosis *Histoplasma capsulatum (cont.)*	4. Chronic disseminated histoplasmosis with variable symptoms, such as unexplained fever, anemia, patchy pneumonia, mucosal ulcers of the mouth, larynx, stomach, or bowel		
BACTERIAL INFECTIONS			
Typhoid Fever *Salmonella typhi*	Acute enteric fever manifested by sustained bacteremia and microabscess formation and ulceration of the distal ileum Gastrointestinal symptoms generally follow the systemic manifestations	1–3 wk	Culture of urine and/or stool positive for *Salmonella typhi* during 2nd wk Culture of blood positive for *S. typhi* during 1st wk Leukopenia Anemia

••

Management	Complications	Nursing Considerations
IV fluids and electrolytes Bed rest Avoid antispasmodics, laxatives, and salicylates. Chloramphenicol (Chloromycetin) or ampicillin (Omnipen) either IV or PO Immunization is advised for travelers to areas of high endemicity. Ampicillin may terminate the chronic carrier state and is preferred in intravascular infection.	Endocarditis Meningitis Pneumonia Pyelonephritis Osteomyelitis Intestinal perforation and hemorrhage Septicemia	1. Transmitted by contaminated food or water and via direct fecal–oral route 2. Relapses occur in 5–10% of untreated cases and may be more common following antibiotic therapy. Report symptoms immediately. 3. Instruct patient to wash hands thoroughly after defecation and before preparing food. 4. Family and close contacts should be examined and treated. 5. Typhoid is communicable for as long as the infective organism is in the feces or urine, which may persist for up to 1 year.

(continued)

TABLE 10-10 Selected Infectious Diseases
(Continued)

Disease and Infectious Agent	Clinical Manifestations	Incubation Period	Diagnostic Tests
Botulism *Clostridium botulinum*	Severe intoxication characterized by visual difficulty, dysphagia, and dry mouth followed by descending symmetrical flaccid paralysis Vomiting and constipation or diarrhea may be present initially.	12–36 h, sometimes several days after eating contaminated food	Culture of *C. botulinum* from stool or stomach contents Serum positive for botulinal toxins
Tetanus *Clostridium tetani*	Acute disease induced by an exotoxin of the tetanus bacillus Painful muscular contractions, primarily of the masseter and neck muscles Abdominal rigidity Generalized spasms frequently induced by sensory stimuli—opisthotonos (arching of the trunk) and risus sardonicus (distorted grin)	Usually 3–21 d; average 3–10 d	Organism rarely recovered from the site of infection No detectable antibody response
Staphylococci *Staphylococcus aureus* Coagulase-negative staphylococci; *S. epidermidis, S. haemolyticus*	Skin and soft tissue infections—furuncles (boils), impetigo, carbuncles, cellulitis, abscesses,	Variable; usually 4–10 d	Confirmed by isolation of the organism from culture

Management	Complications	Nursing Considerations
IV and IM administration of trivalent botulinum antitoxin as soon as possible IV fluids and electrolytes Intensive care to anticipate and manage respiratory failure: mechanical ventilation Report to health department immediately.	Death from respiratory failure	1. All patient contacts known to have eaten the same food should have gastric lavage, high enemas, and cathartics and should be kept under close medical supervision. 2. Instruct patient/patient contacts to wash hands thoroughly after defecation and before handling food. 3. No questionable canned food should ever be tasted.
High case fatality rate 30–90% Tetanus immune globulin Wound care to include cleaning and irrigation Sedatives and muscle relaxants Neuromuscular blockade for treatment of severe uncontrolled spasms (pancurmonium [Pavulon]) Cardiac monitoring Sympathetic blocking agents for management of hypertension and tachycardia (propranolol [Inderal])	Cardiac arrest Bacterial shock Autonomic disturbances	1. Refer persons with skin injuries for tetanus prophylaxis. 2. Remind adults to receive a tetanus booster every 10 years.
Penicillinase-resistant penicillins (nafcillin [Unipen]) and the cephalosporins (cephalothin [Keflin]) Vancomycin (Vancocin) is	Septicemia Embolic skin lesions Death	1. Monitor patient's response to prescribed therapy. 2. Emphasize meticulous hand washing among patients and visitors.

(continued)

TABLE 10-10 Selected Infectious Diseases (Continued)

Disease and Infectious Agent	Clinical Manifestations	Incubation Period	Diagnostic Tests
Staphylococci *Staphylococcus aureus* Coagulase-negative staphylococci; *S. epidermidis, S. haemolyticus* (cont.)	and infected lacerations Seeding of the bloodstream may lead to pneumonia, osteomyelitis, septicemia, endocarditis, meningitis, hepatic abscess, splenic abscess, perinephritic abscess.		
Streptococci *Streptococcus pyogenes,* group A with approximately 80 serologically distinct types	Streptococcal pharyngitis Wound and skin infections— impetigo, cellulitis, erysipelas Scarlet fever (strep-tococcal sore throat with a rash that occurs if infectious agent produces erythrogenic toxin to which patient is not immune)	Short; usually 1–3 d	Identification of group A strepto-coccal antigen in pharyngeal secretions (rapid strep test) Isolation of the organism by culture
Syphilis (*Treponema pallidum,* a sexually trans-mitted infection)	Primary: indurated, painless, clean ulcer (chancre); may be bilateral inguinal adenopathy Secondary: macular-papular rash including palms and	Usually 3 wk, but may be up to 3 mo; signs of secondary syphilis de-velop about 6 wk after healing of chancre.	Nonspecific sero-logic tests such as RPR and VDRL; con-firmed by spe-cific antitrep-onemal antibody tests such as FTA-ABS and MHA-TP; dark-field

Management	Complications	Nursing Considerations
treatment of choice for methicillin-resistant *S. aureus.* Incision of abscesses to permit drainage of pus In severe systemic infection, the selection of antibiotics should be governed by results of susceptibility tests on the isolates.		3. Contain purulent drainage with a dressing. 4. Place soiled dressings in a paper bag before disposal.
Penicillin (Betapen-VK) is the drug of choice. Therapy should be continued for at least 10 days. Erythromycin (Eryc) for penicillin-allergic patients.	Septicemia Acute glomerulonephritis Rheumatic fever	1. Repeated attacks of sore throat or other streptococcal disease due to different types of streptococci are relatively frequent. 2. Make sure the patient understands the importance of completing the course of antimicrobial therapy. 3. Emphasize the relationship of strepococcal infections to heart disease and glomerulonephritis.
Primary and secondary: benzathine penicillin (Bicillin LA) G 2.4 million units IM in a single dose; in penicillin allergy, if not pregnant, doxycycline 100 mg, bid for 2 weeks; erythromycin is an inferior substitute in pregnant, penicillin-	Tertiary syphilis with cardiac, dermatologic, neurologic, and other systemic manifestations	1. Warn patient of possible Jarisch-Herxheimer reaction—fever, myalgias, headache, hypotension—within 24 h of treatment. 2. Ensure that sexual activity is not resumed until treatment is complete for both patient

(continued)

TABLE 10-10 Selected Infectious Diseases
(Continued)
••

Disease and Infectious Agent	Clinical Manifestations	Incubation Period	Diagnostic Tests
Syphilis (*Treponema pallidum,* a sexually trans- mitted infection) *(cont.)*	soles; fever; generalized adenopathy, condyloma lata		examination of lesion exudate for organism

••

Management	Complications	Nursing Considerations
allergic patients		and partner.
		3. Consider testing for HIV and other sexually transmitted diseases.
		4. Encourage follow-up at 3 mo for repeat serologic testing.

IV: intravenous SGOT: serum glutamic oxaloacetic transaminase; PO: by mouth; BID: twice daily; WBC: white blood cell; ASA: acetylsalicylic acid; CNS: central nervous system; GI: gastrointestinal; CSF: cerebrospinal fluid; RBC: red blood cell.

TABLE 10-11 Bone Marrow Aspiration*

Formed Cell Elements	Normal Mean (%)	Range (%)
Undifferentiated cells	0.0	0.0–1.0
Reticulum cells	0.4	0.0–1.3
Myeloblasts	2.0	0.3–5.0
Promyelocytes	5.0	1.0–8.0
Myelocytes		
Neutrophilic	12.0	5.0–19.0
Eosinophilic	1.5	0.5–3.0
Basophilic	0.3	0.0–0.5
Metamyelocytes		
Neutrophilic	25.6	17.5–33.7
Eosinophilic	1.5	0.5–3.0
Basophilic	0.3	0.0–0.5
Metamyelocytes		
Neutrophilic	25.6	17.5–33.7
Eosinophilic	0.4	0.0–1.0
Basophilic	0.0	0.0–0.2
Segmented granulocytes		
Neutrophilic	20.0	11.6–30.0
Eosinophilic	2.0	0.5–4.0
Basophilic	0.2	0.0–3.7
Monocytes	2.0	1.6–4.3
Lymphocytes	10.0	3.0–2.4
Megakaryocytes	0.4	0.0–3.0
Plasma cells	0.9	0.0–2.0
Erythroid series		
Pronormoblasts	0.5	0.2–4.2
Basophilic normoblasts	1.6	0.25–4.8
Polychromatic normoblasts	10.4	3.5–20.5
Orthochromatic normoblasts	6.4	3.0–25
Promegaloblasts	0	0
Basophilic megaloblasts	0	0
Polychromatic megaloblasts	0	0
Orthochromatic megaloblasts	0	0
Myeloid/erythroid ratio (M/E) ratio of WBC to nucleated RBC	2:1–4:1	

* Normal values. (These values are only for adults.)

TABLE 10-12 Hemogram*

Age	WBC × 10³	RBC × 10⁶	Hb g/dL	HCT (%)	MCV fl
Birth–2 wk	9.0–30.0	4.1–6.1	14.5–24.5	44–64	
2–8 wk	2.0–21.0	4.0–6.0	12.5–20.5	39–59	98–112
2–6 mo	5.0–19.0	3.8–5.6	10.7–17.3	35–49	83–97
6 mo–1 y	5.0–19.0	3.8–5.2	9.9–14.5	29–43	73–87
1–6 y	5.0–19.0	3.9–5.3	9.5–14.1	30–40	70–84
6–16 y	4.8–10.8	4.0–5.2	10.3–14.9	32–42	73–87
16–18 y	4.8–10.8	4.2–5.4	11.1–15.7	34–44	75–89
>18 y					
males	5.0–10.0	4.5–5.5	14.0–17.4	42–52	84–96
females	5.0–10.0	4.0–5.0	12.0–16.0	36–48	

Age	MCH pg	MCHC g/dL	PLTS × 10³	RDW (%)	MPV fl
Birth–2 wk	34–40	33–37	150–450		
2–8 wk	30–36	32–36			
2–6 mo	27–33	31–35			
6 mo–1 y	24–30	32–36			
1–6 y	23–29	31–35			
6–16 y	24–30	32–36			
16–18 y	25–31	32–36			
>18 y	28–34	32–36	140–400	11.5–14.5	7.4–10.4

* Normal values.

Hb: hemoglobin; HCT: hematocrit; MCH: mean corpuscular hemoglobin; MCHC: mean corpuscular hemoglobin concentration; MCV: mean corpuscular volume; PLTS: platelets; RBC: red blood cells; WBC: white blood cells.

TABLE 10-13 Differential White Blood Cell Count*

Age	Bands (% STAB)	Segs (% VENT)	Eosinophils (%)	Basophils (%)	Lymphocytes (%)	Monocytes (%)	Metamyelocytes (%)
Birth–1 wk	10–18	32–62	0–2	0–1	26–36	0–6	
1–2 wk	8–16	19–49	0–4	0–0	38–46	0–9	
2–4 wk	7–15	14–34	0–3	0–0	43–53	0–9	
4–8 wk	7–13	15–35	0–3	0–1	41–71	0–7	
2–6 mo	5–11	15–35	0–3	0–1	42–72	0–6	
6 mo–1 y	6–12	13–33	0–3	0–0	46–76	0–5	
1–6 y	5–11	13–33	0–3	0–0	46–76	0–5	
6–16 y	5–11	32–54	0–3	0–1	27–57	0–5	
16–18 y	5–11	34–64	0–3	0–1	25–45	0–5	
>18 y	3–6	50–62	0–3	0–1	25–40	3–7	0–1

* Normal values.

TABLE 10-14 Red Blood Cell Count (RBC; Erythrocyte Count)

••

Normal Values:

Men: $4.2–5.4 \times 10^6/\mu L$ (average 4.8) or $4.2–5.4 \times 10^{12}/L$

Women: $3.6–5.0 \times 10^6/\mu L$ (average 4.3) or $3.6–5.0 \times 10^{12}/L$

Age	RBC $\times$ 10^6
Birth–2 wk	4.1–6.1
2–8 wk	4.0–6.0
2–6 mo	3.8–5.6
6 mo–1 y	3.8–5.2
1–6 y	3.9–5.3
6–16 y	4.0–5.2
16–18 y	4.2–5.4
>18 y	
males	4.5–5.5
females	4.0–5.0

••

TABLE 10-15 Hemoglobin (Hb)*

••

Adult	
Female	12.0–16.0 g/dL, or 1.86–2.48 nmol/L
Male	14.0–17.4 g/dL
Child	
0–2 wk	14.5–24.5 g/dL
2–8 wk	12.5–20.5 g/dL
2–6 mo	10.7–17.3 g/dL
6 mo–1 y	9.9–14.5 g/dL
1–6 y	9.5–14.1 g/dL
6–16 y	10.3–14.9 g/dL
16–18 y	11.1–15.7 g/dL

••

* Normal values.

TABLE 10-16 Hematocrit*

	Percentage
ADULT	
Female	36–48
Male	42–52
CHILD	
0–2 wk	44–64
2–8 wk	39–59
2–6 mo	35–49
6 mo–1 y	29–43
1–6 y	30–40
6–16 y	32–42
16–18 y	34–44

* Normal values.

TABLE 10-17 Coagulant Factor Assay*

Factor II: 80%–120% of normal
Factor V: 50%–150% of normal
Factor VII: 65%–140% of normal or 65–135 AU
Factor VIII: 55%–145% of normal or 55–145 AU
Factor IX: 60%–140% of normal or 60–140 AU
Factor X: 45%–155% of normal or 45–155 AU
Factor XI: 65%–135% of normal or 65–135 AU
Factor XII: 50%–150% of normal or 50–150 AU
Ristocetin–von Willebrand factor: 45%–140% of normal or 45–140 AU
Factor VIII antigen: 50–150 mg/dL
Factor VIII–related antigen: 45%–185% of normal or 45–185 AU
Fletcher factor (prekallikrein): 80%–120% of normal

* Normal values.

TABLE 10-18 Quantitative Immunoglobulins

NORMAL VALUES IN ADULTS

IgG: 700–1500 mg/dL for men and women ≥18 years of age
IgA: 60–400 mg/dL for men and women ≥18 years of age
IgM: 60–300 mg/dL for men and women ≥18 years of age
These values are derived from rate nephelometry.

NORMAL VALUES IN CHILDREN

(Results reported in mg/dL; ranges ±250)

IgA (Males and Females)

0–4 mo	5–64
5–8 mo	10–87
9–14 mo	17–94
15–23 mo	22–178
2–3 y	24–192
4–6 y	26–232
7–9 y	33–258
10–12 y	45–285
13–15 y	47–317
16–17 y	55–377

IgG (Males and Females)

0–4 mo	141–930
5–8 mo	250–1190
9–11 mo	320–1250
1–3 y	400–1250
4–6 y	560–1307
7–9 y	598–1379
10–12 y	638–1453
13–15 y	680–1531
16–17 y	724–1611

IgM (Males)

0–4 mo	14–142
5–8 mo	24–167
9–23 mo	35–200
2–3 y	41–200
4–17 y	47–200

IgM (Females)

0–4 mo	14–142
5–8 mo	24–167
9–23 mo	35–242
2–3 y	41–242
4–17 y	56–242

TABLE 10-19 Lymphocyte Immunophenotyping

NORMAL VALUES OF ADULT PERIPHERAL BLOOD BY FLOW CYTOMETRY

T and B Surface Markers

Cells	Percentage (%)
Total T cells (CD3)	53–88
T-helper cells (CD3$^+$, CD4$^+$)	32–61
T-suppressor cells (CD3$^+$, CD8$^+$)	18–42
B cells (CD19)	5–20
Natural killer cells (CD16)	4–32

Absolute Counts (Based on Pathologist's Interpretation)

Cells	Number of Cells (µL)
Lymphocytes	$0.66–4.60 \times 10^3$
Total T cells (CD3)	812–2318
T-helper cells (CD3$^+$, CD4$^+$)	589–1505
T-suppressor cells (CD3$^+$, CD8$^+$)	325–997
B cells (CD19)	92–426
Natural killer cells (CD16)	78–602

Lymphocyte Ratio

T-helper–T-suppressor > 1.0

CHAPTER 11

Musculoskeletal Reference Facts

TABLE 11-1 Divisions of the Skeleton
....

AXIAL

Skull
   Cranial bones
   Facial bones
   Ossicles
   Hyoid
Vertebral column
   Vertebrae
   Intervertebral disks
   Sacrum
   Coccyx
Thoracic cage
   Ribs
   Sternum
   Costal cartilages

APPENDICULAR

Extremities
   Arms
      Humerus
      Radius
      Ulna
      Carpals
      Metacarpals
      Phalanges
   Legs
      Femur
      Patella
      Tibia
      Fibula
      Tarsals
      Metatarsals
      Phalanges
Shoulder
   Scapulae
   Clavicle
Pelvic girdle
   Os coxae (3 fused hip bones)
   Symphysis pubis

....

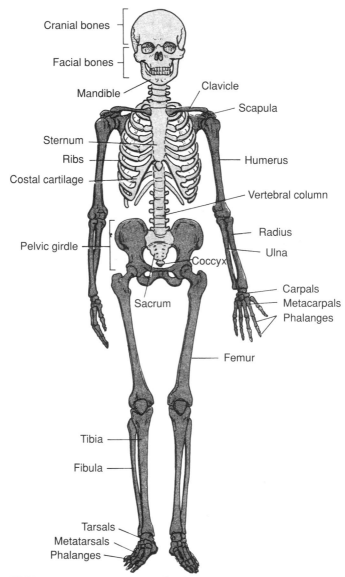

FIGURE 11-1 Major bones in the skeleton.

TABLE 11-2 The Vertebral Column

Cervical–C1 to C7
Thoracic–T1 to T12
Lumbar–L1 to L5
Sacrum–S1 to S5
Coccyx

TABLE 11-3 Major Muscles in the Body

Muscle	Location*	Action	Notes
Neck and Shoulders			
Sternocleidomastoid	Side of neck	Helps keep head erect	If diseased or injured, head is permanently drawn to one side (torticollis).
Deltoid	Shoulder	Moves upper arm outward from body	Site for intramuscular injections
Arm and Anterior Chest			
Biceps	Front of upper arms	Flexes forearm	
Triceps	Posterior to biceps	Extends forearm	
Pectoralis major ⎫	Anterior upper portion of chest	Help to bring arms across chest	
Pectoralis minor ⎬	Anterior chest, arising from ribs		
Serratus anterior ⎭			
Respiration			
Diaphragm	Between the abdominal and thoracic cavities	Assists in process of breathing	When it contracts, it moves downward, making chest cavity larger, forming a partial vacuum around the lungs and causing air to rush into them. When it relaxes, it pushes upward and air is forced out of the lungs.

Muscle	Location	Action	Notes
Intercostal	Between the ribs	Helps to enlarge the chest cavity (side to side and back to front)	Same actions as above
Abdomen Internal oblique External oblique Transversus abdominis Rectus abdominis	Flat bands that stretch from ribs to pelvis, overlapping in layers from various angles	Support abdominal organs	An opening in muscle creates weakness where a hernia (rupture) may occur.
Back and Posterior Chest Trapezius dorsi Latissimus dorsi and other back muscles	Across back and posterior chest Across back and posterior chest	Helps to lift shoulder Work in groups; help to stand erect, balance when heavy objects are carried, and turn or bend body; adduct upper arm	Also called "swimming muscle"
Gluteal Gluteus maximus Gluteus medius Gluteus minimus	Form the buttocks	Help change from sitting to standing position; help in walking	Frequently used as site for intramuscular injections
Thigh and Lower Leg Quadriceps femoris group Rectus femoris Vastus lateralis Vastus intermedius Vastus medialis	Anterior thigh	Extend leg and thigh	Rectus femoris and vastus lateralis used as injection sites

(continued)

247

TABLE 11-3 Major Muscles in the Body (Continued)

Muscle	Location*	Action	Notes
Hamstring group Biceps femoris Semimembranosus Semitendinosus	Posterior thigh	Flexes and extends leg and thigh	
Gracilis	Thigh	Flexes and adducts leg; adducts thigh	
Sartorius	Thigh	Flexes and rotates thigh and leg	Called "tailor's muscle" because it allows sitting in cross-legged position
Tibialis anterior	Anterior lower leg	Elevates and flexes foot	

Muscle	Location	Function	Notes
Gastrocnemius	Calf	Flexes foot and leg	Give calf rounded appearance
Soleus	Calf	Extends and rotates foot	
Peroneus longus	Calf	Extends, abducts, and everts foot	
Achilles tendon	Attaches calf muscles to heel bone	Allows extension of foot and gives "spring" to walk	Term derived from Greek mythology
Head			
Orbicularis oculi	Head	Move eyes and wrinkle forehead	Disorder may cause strabismus ("cross-eye")
Orbicularis oris	Head	Moves mouth and surrounding facial structures	
Masseter	Head	Assists in chewing by raising lower jaw	
Buccinator	Head	Moves fleshy portion of cheek for smiling	

* For placement of these muscles, see Figure 11-2.

ANTERIOR VIEW

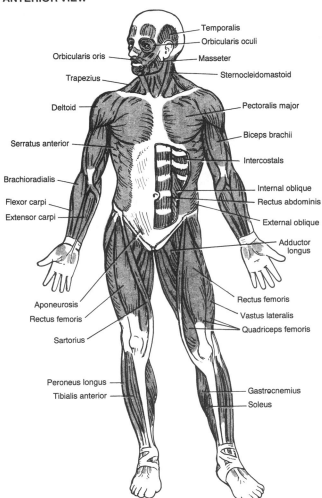

FIGURE 11-2 Major muscles in the body.

POSTERIOR VIEW

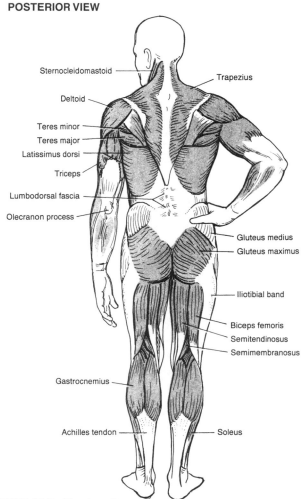

Sternocleidomastoid

Trapezius

Deltoid

Teres minor

Teres major

Latissimus dorsi

Triceps

Lumbodorsal fascia

Olecranon process

Gluteus medius

Gluteus maximus

Iliotibial band

Biceps femoris

Semitendinosus

Semimembranosus

Gastrocnemius

Achilles tendon

Soleus

FIGURE 11-2 (Continued)

TABLE 11-4 Joint Types

Type of Joint	Description
Ball-and-socket joint	Rounded head of one bone fits into a cuplike cavity in the other; flexion–extension, abduction–adduction, and rotation are permitted (eg, shoulder and hip joints).
Condyloid joint	Oval head of one bone fits into a shallow cavity of another bone; flexion–extension and abduction–adduction are permitted (eg, wrist joint).
Gliding joint	Articular surfaces are flat; flexion–extension and abduction–adduction are permitted (eg, carpal bones of wrist and tarsal bones of feet).
Hinge joint	Spool-like surface fits into a concave surface; only flexion–extension is permitted (eg, elbow, knee, and ankle joints).
Pivot joint	Ringlike structure that turns on a pivot; movement is limited to rotation, for example, turning a doorknob (eg, joints between the atlas and axis and between the proximal ends of the radius and the ulna).
Saddle joint	Bone surfaces are convex on one side and concave on the other; movements are side to side and back and forth (eg, joint between the trapezium and metacarpal of the thumb).

TABLE 11-5 Terms Used to Describe Body Movements

Term	Definition and Example
Abduction	Lateral movement of a body part away from the midline of the body. *Example:* A person's arm is abducted when it is moved away from the body.
Adduction	Lateral movement of a body part toward the midline of the body. *Example:* A person's arm is adducted when it is moved from an outstretched position to a position alongside the body.
Circumduction	Movement of the distal part of the limb to trace a complete circle while the proximal end of the bone remains fixed. *Example:* The leg is outstretched and moved in a circle.
Flexion	The state of being bent. *Example:* A person's cervical spine is flexed when the head is bent forward chin to chest.

TABLE 11-5 Terms Used to Describe Body Movements (Continued)

Term	Definition and Example
Extension	The state of being in a straight line. *Example:* A person's cervical spine is extended when the head is held straight on the spinal column.
Hyperextension	The state of exaggerated extension. It often results in an angle greater than 180 degrees. *Example:* A person's cervical spine is hyperextended when looking overhead, toward the ceiling.
Dorsiflexion	Backward bending of the hand or foot. *Example:* A person's foot is in dorsiflexion when the toes are brought up as though to point them at the knee.
Plantar flexion	Flexion of the foot. *Example:* A person's foot is in plantar flexion in the footdrop position.
Rotation	Turning on an axis; the turning of a body part on the axis provided by its joint. *Example:* A thumb is rotated when it is moved to make a circle.
Internal rotation	A body part turning on its axis toward the midline of the body. *Example:* A leg is rotated internally when it turns inward at the hip and the toes point toward the midline of the body.
External rotation	A body part turning on its axis away from the midline of the body. *Example:* A leg is rotated externally when it turns outward at the hip and the toes point away from the midline of the body.

SPECIAL MOVEMENTS

Term	Definition and Example
Pronation	The assumption of the prone position. *Examples:* A person is in the prone position when lying on the abdomen; a person's palm is prone when the forearm is turned so that the palm faces downward.
Supination	The assumption of the supine position. *Examples:* A person is in the supine position when lying on the back; a person's palm is supine when the forearm is turned so that the palm faces upward.
Inversion	Movement of the sole of the foot inward (occurs at the ankle)
Eversion	Movement of the sole of the foot outward (occurs at the ankle)

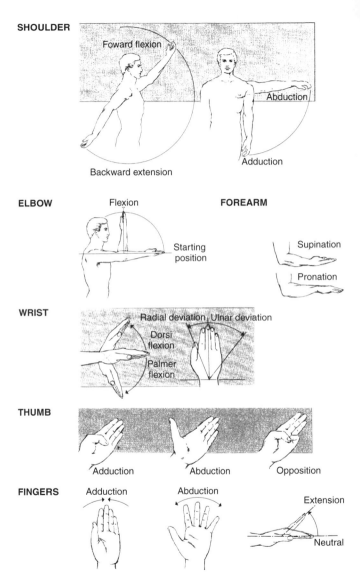

FIGURE 11-3 Range of motion.

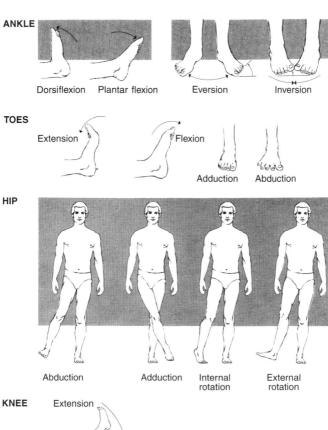

ANKLE

Dorsiflexion   Plantar flexion   Eversion   Inversion

TOES

Extension   Flexion

Adduction   Abduction

HIP

Abduction   Adduction   Internal   External
                                rotation   rotation

KNEE   Extension

Flexion

Figure continued on following page

FIGURE 11-3 (Continued)

CERVICAL SPINE

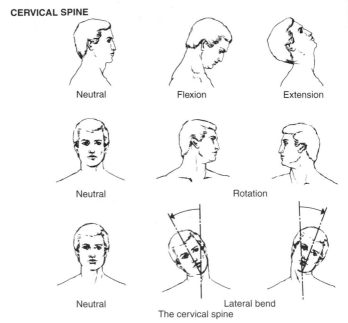

Neutral   Flexion   Extension

Neutral   Rotation

Neutral   Lateral bend

The cervical spine

FIGURE 11-3 (Continued)

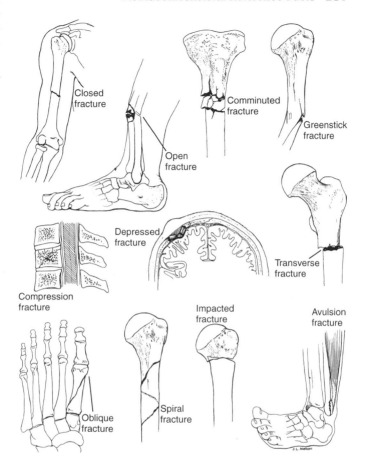

FIGURE 11-4 Types of fractures.

CHAPTER 12

Integumentary
Reference Facts

TABLE 12-1 Skin Color Assessment

Color Variations	Assessment Areas	Pathologic Causes
Redness (erythema; flushing)	Facial area, localized area	Blushing, alcohol intake, fever, injury trauma, infection
Bluish (cyanosis)	Exposed areas, particularly the ears, lips, inside of the mouth, hands and feet, nailbeds	Cold environment, cardiac or respiratory disease (decreased oxygenation)
Yellowish (jaundice)	Overall skin areas, mucous membranes, and sclera	Liver disease (increase in bilirubin levels)
Paleness (pallor)	Exposed areas, particularly the face and lips, conjunctivae, and mucous membranes	Anemia (decreased hemoglobin)
	Overall skin areas, lips, nailbeds, conjunctivae	Shock (decreased blood volume)
Vitiligo	Whitish patchy areas on the skin	Depigmentation (congenital or autoimmune conditions)
Tanned or brown	Sun-exposed areas	Overexposure (increased melanin production), pregnancy (brown spots?)

PRIMARY SKIN LESIONS

Primary skin lesions are original lesions arising from previously normal skin. Secondary lesions can originate from primary lesions.

Macule
Patch

MACULE, PATCH
- Macule: <1cm, circumscribed border
- Patch: >1cm, may have irregular border
- Flat, nonpalpable skin color change (color may be brown, white, tan, purple, red)

Examples:

Freckles, flat moles, petechia, rubella, vitiligo, port wine stains, ecchymosis

PAPULE, PLAQUE
- Papule: <0.5 cm   Papule
- Plaque: >0.5 cm
- Elevated, palpable, solid mass   Plaque
- Circumscribed border
- Plaque may be coalesced papules with flat top

Examples:

Papules: Elevated nevi, warts, lichen planus
Plaques: Psoriasis, actinic keratosis

NODULE, TUMOR
- Nodule: 0.5–2 cm
- Tumor: >1–2 cm
- Elevated, palpable, solid mass   Tumor
- Extends deeper into dermis than a papule
- Nodules circumscribed
- Tumors do not always have sharp borders

Examples:
Nodules: Lipoma, squamous cell carcinoma, poorly absorbed injection, dermatofibroma

Tumors: Larger lipoma, carcinoma

VESICLE, BULLA   Bulla   Vesicle
- Vesicle: <0.5 cm
- Bulla: >0.5 cm
- Circumscribed, elevated, palpable mass containing serous fluid

Examples:

Vesicles: Herpes simplex/zoster, chickenpox, poison ivy, second-degree burn (blister)

Bulla: Pemphigus, contact dermatitis, large burn blisters, poison ivy, bullous impetigo

WHEAL
- Elevated mass with transient borders
- Often irregular   Wheal
- Size, color vary
- Caused by movement of serous fluid into the dermis
- Does not contain free fluid in a cavity as, for example, a vesicle

Examples:

Urticaria (hives), insect bites

PUSTULE
- Pus-filled vesicle or bulla

Examples: Pustule

Acne, impetigo, furuncles, carbuncles

CYST
- Encapsulated fluid-filled or semi-soild mass
- In the subcutaneous tissue or dermis

Examples:

Sebaceous cyst, epidermoid cyst   Cyst

FIGURE 12-1 Types of skin lesions.

SECONDARY SKIN LESIONS

Secondary skin lesions result from changes in primary lesions.

EROSION
- Loss of superficial epidermis
- Does not extend to dermis
- Depressed, moist area

Erosion

Examples:

Ruptured vesicles, scratch marks

ULCER
- Skin loss extending past epidermis
- Necrotic tissue loss
- Bleeding and scarring possible

Ulcer

Examples:

Stasis ulcer of venous insufficiency, decubitus ulcer

FISSURE
- Linear crack in the skin
- May extend to dermis

Fissure

Examples:

Chapped lips or hands, athlete's foot

SCALES
- Flakes secondary to desquamated, dead epithelium
- Flakes may adhere to skin surface
- Color varies (silvery, white)
- Texture varies (thick, fine)

Scales

Examples:

Dandruff, psoriasis, dry skin, pityriasis rosea

CRUST
- Dried residue of serum, blood or pus on skin surface
- Large adherent crust is a scab

Crust

Examples:

Residue left after vesicle rupture: impetigo, herpes, eczema

SCAR (Cicatrix)
- Skin mark left after healing of a wound or lesion

Scar

- Represents replacement by connective tissue of the injured tissue
- Young scars: red or purple
- Mature scars: white or glistening

Example:
Healed wound or surgical incision

KELOID
- Hypertrophied scar tissue

Keloid

- Secondary to excessive collagen formation during healing
- Elevated, irregular, red
- Greater incidence in blacks

Example:

Keloid of ear piercing or surgical incision

ATROPHY
- Thin, dry, transparent appearance of epidermis

Atrophy

- Secondary to loss of collagen and elastin
- Underlying vessels may be visible

Examples:

Aged skin, arterial insufficiency

LICHENIFICATION
- Thickening and roughening of the skin

Lichenification

- Accentuated skin markings
- May be secondary to repeated rubbing, irritation, scratching

Example:
Contact dermatitis

FIGURE 12-1 (Continued)

TABLE 12-2 Types of Wounds

Wound	Description
BROAD CATEGORIES	
Accidental	Unintentional injury, such as knife, gunshot, burn; jagged edges; bleeding; unsterile
Surgical	Planned therapy, such as surgical incision, needle introduction; clean edges; controlled bleeding; controlled surgical asepsis
SKIN INTEGRITY	
Open	Break in skin or mucous membranes; may bleed with tissue damage; infection risk
Closed	No break in skin integrity, but soft tissue damage present; may have internal injury and bleeding
DESCRIPTORS	
Abrasion	Wound involving friction of skin; superficial; dermatologic procedure for scar tissue removal
Puncture	Intentional or unintentional penetrating trauma; made by sharp instrument that penetrates skin and underlying tissue
Laceration	Ragged wound edges with torn tissues; object may be contaminated; infection risk
Contusion	Closed wound; bleeding in underlying tissues caused by blunt blow; bruise
CLASSIFICATIONS OF SURGICAL WOUNDS	
Clean	Closed surgical wound that did not enter gastrointestinal, respiratory, or genitourinary systems; low infection risk
Clean/contaminated	Wound entering gastrointestinal, respiratory, or genitourinary systems; infection risk
Contaminated	Open, traumatic wound; surgical wound with break in asepsis; high infection risk
Infected	Wound site with pathogens present; signs of infection

Primary Intention (Primary union)

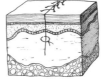

Clean incision   Early suture   "Hairline" scar

Secondary Intention (contraction and epithelialization) (Granulation)

Gaping irregular wound   Granulation   Epithelium grows over scar

Tertiary Intention (delayed closure)

Wound   Granulation   Closure with wide scar

FIGURE 12-2 Stages of wound healing.

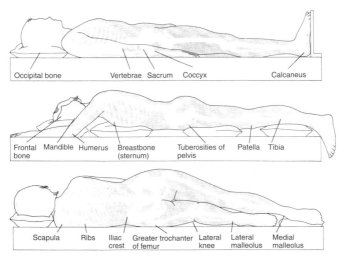

Occipital bone   Vertebrae Sacrum Coccyx   Calcaneus

Frontal bone   Mandible Humerus   Breastbone (sternum)   Tuberosities of pelvis   Patella   Tibia

Scapula   Ribs   Iliac crest   Greater trochanter of femur   Lateral knee   Lateral malleolus   Medial malleolus

FIGURE 12-3 Common pressure points.

Stage 4
Necrosis will extend through the fascia and may even involve the bone. Eschar is a common finding. Bone destruction can lead to periosteitis, osteitis, and osteomyelitis.

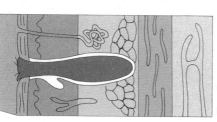

Stage 3
There is an open lesion and a crater exposing sub-cutaneous tissue. You may be able to see fascia at the base of the ulcer.

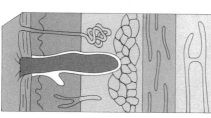

Stage 2
Redness persists, usually accompanied by edema and induration. The epidermis may blister or erode.

Stage 1
The primary sign is redness. The skin doesn't return to a normal color when the pressure is relieved, but there is no induration—the skin and underlying tissues remain soft.

FIGURE 12-4 Stages of pressure ulcers.

TABLE 12-3 Common Types of Drains

Type	Purpose	Example
Penrose	Provides sinus tract	After incision and drainage of abscess, in abdominal surgery
T-tube	For bile drainage	After gallbladder surgery
Jackson-Pratt	Decrease dead space by collecting drainage	After breast removal, abdominal surgery
Hemovac	Decrease dead space by collecting drainage	After abdominal, orthopedic surgery
Gauze, iodoform gauze, Nu Gauze	Allow healing from base of wound	Infected wounds, after removal of hemorrhoids

TABLE 12-4 Temperatures for Heat and Cold Applications

Description	Temperature Range	Example
Very cold	<59°F (15°C)	Ice bags
Cold	59°–65°F (15°–18°C)	Cold pack
Cool	65°–80°F (18°–27°C)	Cold compress
Tepid	80°–98°F (27°–37°C)	Alcohol sponge bath
Warm	98°–105°F (37°–41°C)	Aquathermia (Aqua-K) pad
Hot	105°–115°F (41°–46°C)	Hot soak
Very hot	115°F (46°C)	Hot water bottle

TABLE 12-5 Burn Characteristics

Depth	Tissues Involved	Usual Cause	Characteristics	Pain	Healing
Superficial partial-thickness (first degree)	Minimal epithelial damage	Sun	Dry No blisters Pinkish red Blanches with pressure	Painful	About 5 days
Superficial partial-thickness (second degree)	Epidermis, minimal dermis	Flash Hot liquids	Moist Pinkish or mottled red Blisters Some blanching	Pain Hyperesthetic	About 21 days, minimal scarring
Deep dermal partial-thickness (second degree)	Entire epidermis, part of dermis, epidermal-lined hair and sweat glands intact	Above plus hot solids, flame, and intense radiant injury	Dry, pale, waxy No blanching	Sensitive to pressure	Prolonged; late hypertrophic scarring; marked contracture formation
Full-thickness (third degree)	All of above, and portion of subcutaneous fat; may involve connective tissue, muscle, bone	Sustained flame, electrical, chemical, and steam	Leathery, cracked avascular, pale yellow to brown to charred	Little pain	Cannot self-regenerate; needs grafting

(From Burgess C. Initial management of a patient with extensive burn injury. Critical Care Nursing Clinics of North America 3(2):167, 1991.)

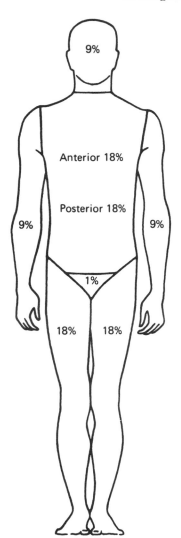

FIGURE 12-5 Rule of nines.

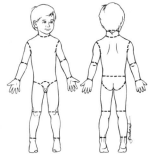

Age-Years

Area	0–1	1–4	5–9	10–15	Adult	% 2	% 3	% Total
Head	19	17	13	10	7			
Neck	2	2	2	2	2			
Ant. Trunk	13	13	13	13	13			
Post. Trunk	13	13	13	13	13			
R. Buttock	2	2	2	2	2			
L. Buttock	2	2	2	2	2			
Genitalia	1	1	1	1	1			
R. U. Arm	4	4	4	4	4			
L. U. Arm	4	4	4	4	4			
R. L. Arm	3	3	3	3	3			
L. L. Arm	3	3	3	3	3			
R. Hand	2	2	2	2	2			
L. Hand	2	2	2	2	2			
R. Thigh	5	6	8	8	9			
L. Thigh	5	6	8	8	9			
R. Leg	5	5	5	6	7			
L. Leg	5	5	5	6	7			
R. Foot	3	3	3	3	3			
L. Foot	3	3	3	3	3			
					Total			

FIGURE 12-6 Lund and Browder chart.

Credits

From Craven RF, Hirnle CJ: *Fundamentals of Nursing*, 1st Edition, Philadelphia, J.B. Lippincott Company, 1992: *Figure* 12-1

From Craven RF, Hirnle CJ: *Fundamentals of Nursing*, 2nd Edition, Philadelphia, Lippincott–Raven Publishers, 1996: *Tables* 1-1, 1-2, 1-5, 1-6, 1-8, 3-2, 5-1, 6-1, 7-2, 12-2 *Figures* 8-1, 12-2

From Fischbach FT: *Manual of Laboratory and Diagnostic Tests*, 5th Edition, Philadelphia, J.B. Lippincott Company, 1995: *Tables* 2-14, 2-15, 4-4, 5-4, 7-3, 8-5, 8-6, 8-7, 9-2, 9-12, 9-13, 9-14, 10-9, 10-11, 10-12, 10-13, 10-14, 10-15, 10-16, 10-17, 10-18, 10-19

From Hudak CM, Gallo BM: *Handbook of Critical Care Nursing*, Philadelphia, J.B. Lippincott Company, 1994: *Tables* 3-4, 3-6, 4-1, 4-2, 5-3, 8-3, 8-4, 12-5 *Figure* 12-5

From *The Lippincott Manual of Nursing Practice*, 6th Edition, Philadelphia, Lippincott–Raven Publishers, 1996: *Tables* 1-4, 1-7, 2-2, 2-3, 2-10, 2-12, 3-3, 3-7, 4-1, 5-2, 6-4, 6-5, 6-6, 7-6, 7-7, 8-2, 9-1, 9-3, 9-4, 9-5, 10-1, 10-2, 10-3, 10-4, 10-5, 10-6, 10-7, 10-8, 10-10 *Figures* 5-2, 6-2, 11-3, 11-4, 12-6

From *Lippincott's Nursing Drug Guide 1996*, Philadelphia, J.B. Lippincott Company, 1996: *Tables* 1-9, 2-4, 2-5, 2-6, 2-7, 2-8, 2-9, 2-13 *Figure* 2-1

From Metheny NM: *Fluid and Electrolyte Balance*, 3rd Edition, Lippincott–Raven Publishers, 1996: *Tables* 3-5, 9-9, 9-10, 9-11

From Porth CM: *Pathophysiology*, 4th Edition, J.B. Lippincott Company, 1994: *Tables* 9-6, 9-7, 9-8 *Figure* 5-3

From Rosdahl CB, *Textbook of Basic Nursing*, 6th Edition, Philadelphia, J.B. Lippincott Company, 1995: *Tables* 1-3, 6-3, 11-1, 11-2, 11-3 *Figures* 1-1, 6-1, 11-1, 11-2

From Smeltzer SC, Bare BG: *Brunner and Suddarth's Textbook of Medical Surgical Nursing*, 7th Edition, Philadelphia, J.B. Lippincott Company, 1992: *Figure* 4-5

From Smeltzer SC, Bare BG: *Brunner and Suddarth's Textbook of Medical Surgical Nursing*, 8th Edition, Philadelphia, Lippincott–Raven Publishers, 1996: *Figures* 4-2, 4-3